Microdosing Psyc

A Practical Guide to Upgrade Your Life

By Paul Austin

Microdosing Psychedelics - A Practical Guide to Upgrade Your Life

Library of Congress Cataloguing-in-Publication Data

Austin, Paul 1990-

Title

ISBN

1. *Psychedelic drugs 2. Microdosing Psychedelics 3. Psychedelics and leadership, entrepreneurialism, technology and creativity 4. Psychedelic drugs and depression, anxiety*

Table of Contents

3

Acknowledgements

4

First, to my parents who have supported – without judgment – most of my crazy pursuits, including my current kick to legitimize psychedelic substances.

Second, to the team who helped me write this book: Louis Greenstein, Aaron Kase, and Ed Hingston. Without your contributions, we wouldn't have made it past page 2.

And, finally, to our community at The Third Wave. In the pursuit of changing the conversation around psychedelics, our early community members have stepped out of the fold and led from a place of heart, authenticity, and meaning.

About the Author

Paul is committed to changing the cultural conversation about psychedelics through his platform, The Third Wave.

Because of his work with microdosing, Paul has been featured in Rolling Stone and Business Insider, with additional pieces in the New York Times, Playboy, and Lifehacker.

In June 2015 Paul began his first microdosing protocol. Immediately, he noticed improvements in his energy levels, creativity, and general sense of well-being. The impact of microdosing was so profound on his life that Paul wanted to help others understand how microdosing could be used as a tool for personal growth and understanding.

In speaking publicly about microdosing, Paul hopes to further spur a dialogue about knowledge, learning, and growth at the intersection of microdosing psychedelics and self-optimization.

He resides in Brooklyn, New York and enjoys travel, hiking, and spending time at third wave cafes.

Introduction

For thousands of years, individuals and societies have used psychedelics as an integral part of their human and spiritual development. In the first wave of psychedelic use, shamans in indigenous societies conducted ritualistic ceremonies with the help of plant medicines. The shamans acted as middlemen between the abstract spirit world and the spiritual needs of their fellow community members. Considering the degree of co-dependency between indigenous tribes and nature, plant medicines served as a necessary reminder of the importance of nature in everyday life. While ayahuasca and the Amazon are the most well-known example of this relationship, there are dozens of illustrations the world over, including psilocybin mushrooms in the former Mayan and Aztec empires; peyote in what is now northern Mexico, New Mexico, and Arizona; and Kykeon ceremonies in Ancient Greece and Rome.

For those of you who have dipped into the bountiful water of the psychedelic experience, you likely understand why such substances were used. According to recent research,[iii] psychedelics are substances that consistently induce a mystical experience. While there are other tools we can draw on to initiate such an experience – meditation, fasting, flagellation, extreme sensory deprivation – none are reliable as the psychedelic experience. In working with the mystical experience, indigenous societies cultivated reverence for the earth on which they depended.

It is only in fairly recent times – since the days of Descartes, Frances Bacon, and the onset of scientism and materialist reductionism in the 15th and 16th centuries – that Western culture has turned away from legitimizing non-dual experiences, and placed the majority of our confidence in the scientific method. While such advancements in science and technology have brought tremendous abundance to 21st century life, they have also come with an unfortunate backlash: a sweeping, dramatic disconnection from our essence – an alienation from the Oneness described by philosophers and mystics. Some call it our true nature; others know it as the Godhead. Whatever we name it, the consequences of this disconnection are clear: rising rates of anxiety and depression, the destruction of ecological capital, and a poisonous attachment to money, status, and ego.

The second wave of psychedelics – more commonly known as the "counterculture" – as the first pushback against an ultra-conformist society devoid of any mystery, awe, or reverence. Two events catalyzed the second wave: Albert Hofmann's synthesis of LSD in 1938 and Gordon Wasson's discovery of the "Magic Mushroom" in Oaxaca. Mexico in 1955. In 1957, Wasson published his experience in *Life Magazine* in a photo essay entitled "Seeking the Magic Mushroom." With the publication of this article in a mainstream media resource, the counterculture began. Without going into too many details, the second wave of psychedelics came to an abrupt halt when Richard Nixon began waging the "War on Drugs" in 1971, with the explicit goal of destabilizing the hippie left for political reasons. By putting the lid on psychedelic use, the military-industrial complex continued to integrate its destructive principles and values into the mainstream; many of which were antithetical to the psychedelic experience brought about by the cultural awakening of the 1960s.

However, with the recent advent of the information age brought on by the Internet, more people are "waking up" to the recognition of how imbalanced our Western society has become as a result of these principles and values. With a looming ecological crisis, work dissatisfaction peaking in corporate environments, and depression and anxiety at all time highs, there is a clear recognition that something is wrong.[iii]

In an effort to facilitate self-healing, more individuals are turning to activities such as yoga, mindfulness meditation, hiking, vegetarianism/veganism, and functional fitness based on evolutionary principles (largely through the popularization of Crossfit). This is no coincidence. Whether the trends are conscious or sub-conscious, such activities are becoming more popular for one reason: people want to optimize their physical, emotional, and spiritual health.

Psychedelics are another tool to facilitate such healing. Unfortunately, they have been demonized by the U.S. government (and, as a result, all modern nation-state governments) because the psychedelic experience cultivates principles many believe are in opposition to the "grow-at-all-costs" mindset of modern nation-state governments. Demonization of the psychedelic experience has created a nearly insurmountable cultural stigma, of which ignorance and misinformation are paramount.

But, we have hope. The cultural conversation around psychedelics is beginning to change thanks to research on the efficacy of psychedelics as medicine, well-known individuals (such as Steve Jobs) "coming out" in support of such substances, and the changing dialogue around previous illicit substances like cannabis.

So, where does microdosing fall into this still-evolving history?

At The Third Wave, we believe that microdosing – taking small, sub-perceptual doses of psychedelics such as LSD and psilocybin – will be a driving force for the integration of psychedelics with mainstream society. Already, we have seen examples of scientific research impacting public policy. As research continues, and as prominent individuals "come out of the psychedelic closet," the stigma around these powerful substances will recede and more people will become properly educated about how to utilize psychedelics in an intentional, structured manner.

Humans are irrational creatures. Many of our decisions are not based on a logical thought process. Our "Reptilian Brain" has an abundance of cognitive biases that prevent us from making choices based on pure logic. Society's perception of the utility of psychedelics is a case in point. Considering the documented history, the scientific findings, and the anecdotal reports, it's obvious that we as a society are not thinking logically about their use.

In spreading the word on microdosing, we hope to cultivate awareness about a new wave of psychedelic use: The Third Wave of Psychedelics. Unlike the first and second waves, The Third Wave educates individuals on the responsible and measured use of psychedelic substances for specific purposes. Instead of facilitating pushback against mainstream narratives, the Third Wave of Psychedelics encourages integration to construct new models in society. These models will recognize the inter-connectedness of all things, turning away from the mindless materialism and consumerism that has destroyed the ecological capital on which we rely.

The use of psychedelics will reflect this change in cultural undertones. Unlike the counterculture of the '50s, '60s, and '70s, when psychedelics were used in rejection of mainstream values, microdosing will imbue mainstream society with the values of the psychedelic experience without requiring a complete and total disconnect. In other words, the Second Wave encouraged separation; the Third Wave encourages integration and coming-togetherness.

You are likely reading this book for one of two reasons. Either you are interested in microdosing because of its reported benefits on creativity, innovation, relationships, and energy levels or you are interested in it because you suffer from a Western-model "deficit" (depression, anxiety, ADHD) and all previous solutions didn't line up with your expectations. You've heard microdosing worked for people, and you want to learn more about it.

We have organized this book into two main sections:

If you're generally curious about microdosing, Section 1 is the best place to start. There, we outline the groundwork to help you make a more informed decision about whether or not this practice may be suitable for your specific situation.

Section 2 is for those who have already committed to trying a microdosing regimen and want to get the most out of it. We discuss preparation protocols, how to create an ideal container, and microdosing for leadership and creativity.

My intention in writing this book is to provide the ultimate how-to for those interested in microdosing for specific pursuits. While there are various anecdotal stories, reports, and even books about the microdosing experience, there is yet to be a comprehensive "how-to" guide for those interested in microdosing.

As of now, there is limited research to back some of the assumptions made in this book. As more research comes out, we will update future editions to reflect the advances. In the meantime, we will primarily draw on anecdotal reports from those who have experimented with microdosing to create a comprehensive framework from which you can benefit.

If you enjoy the book, we ask you to please do two things:

1. Share it with a friend (or two) who could benefit from the information contained within
2. Leave a review on Amazon so others understand how this book could have a profound impact and change on their life

---

i

        R. R. Griffiths & W. A. Richards & U. McCann & R. Jesse, "Psilocybin can occasion mystical-type experiences having substantial and sustained personal meaning and spiritual significance," Psychopharmacology, May 2006

ii

        https://www.conference-board.org/publications/publicationdetail.cfm?publicationid=2785&centerId=4

iii

        https://www.ncbi.nlm.nih.gov/pmc/articles/PMC4097914/, Jeff Wilson, Mindful America: The Mutual Transformation of Buddhist Meditation and American Culture

Part I: The Basics of Microdosing

Chapter 1: Raised with Love, Support, and Care

My story is typical of our times. Born and raised in a traditional, Midwestern, suburban home, my family and community espoused the pillar values of Christianity: humility, kindness, support, and love.

My parents went the extra mile to ensure my childhood and adolescence provided every suburban American opportunity available: private violin lessons, excellent public schools, church every Sunday, and "travel" soccer.

But growing up in a deeply Calvinist culture also came with a few caveats.

Drugs? Bad. Sex? Bad. Thinking Different? Real bad.

Three failures and a revelation

Like any normal teenager, I went along with this belief system – until, one day, the unavoidable occurred: my youthful discontent and rebellion intersected with my getting a driver's license, meaning I was free to roam and do as I pleased. So, at the age of 16, in the confines of a concrete hippie hut with three friends, I smoked my first blunt, the first time I ever consumed a psychoactive substance.

While much of my community regarded cannabis consumption as a sure sign of failure, I remember the experience as mostly positive. Despite the undercurrents of paranoia because we were doing something illegal, I enjoyed the giggling and the general sense of euphoria under the influence of this "bad, life-destroying drug."

Over the next couple months, I tried cannabis two more times. Then, the inevitable happened: my parents found out.

Grounded for a month, they told me it was "best" for me. After all, the United States government had properly "educated" them about the dangers and harms of marijuana. It was illegal because it was bad – and it was bad because it was illegal. Smoking weed leads to stupidity and laziness, and eventually to a miserable life of hard drugs and poverty.

Or not.

From that experience, I learned to keep my family life and social life separate. Again, this is nothing new for most teenagers growing up in suburban America. You, the reader, regardless of the generation in which you grew up, likely experienced something similar.

My next "societal failure" came at the age of 19 when I took LSD for the first time. While much of my community deemed this action a disappointment, a "how could you," my internal self finally came alive to the wondrous awe of life, love, and nature. For the first time in my life, I saw through the veil and deep into what really mattered: relationships, community, and love.

We, as humans, are social animals, and when living in modernized, industrialized cities, we experience the deep disconnection of modern life. LSD catalyzed a profound shift in my life, and, as cliched as it sounds, I was never the same again.

My third point of failure was at the age of 20. As a university sophomore, I wanted to make some extra cash. Already exhausting most of my work options, I chose to sell cannabis on the side. This venture went well... until the day the police showed up at my door.

I never got arrested. I never got fingerprinted. Instead, the four cops took $7,000 in cash and eventually let me off the hook.

Traumatized by this experience, I made an internal commitment to excel and thrive. My objective: change the system in which we currently live, and inform my external actions by the profound psychedelic experiences I had at the age of 19 and 20.

I made this vow because I knew my failures were the same failures experienced by so many others who have grown up in our industrialized Western world.

The real failure is when we adjust and adapt to a culture that is built on consumerism, individualism, and the destruction of ecological capital. In other words: my biggest "failure" was an inability to conform to the poisonous values and principles of modern society, including dogmatic religion, rampant consumerism, and normative drug use.

Which is why you're now reading this book.

Without living through these failures I never would have written a book on a taboo topic like psychedelics. In fact, had I chosen to pursue a more conventional lifestyle – the lifestyle of my college and high school friends, the lifestyle of most in their 20s, 30s, and 40s – it would be nigh impossible to step out of the shadows and expose myself as a psychedelic "user."

From rebellion to productive output: learning how to build an online business

Without boring you with too much detail, the reason I can speak out in such a public way about the importance of psychedelic substances is due to a fortunate sequence of events.

My parents, while misguided in their attempts to protect me from the dangerous world of illicit drugs, provided a stable home in which I grew up, overflowing with love, care, and compassion. This went beyond intangibles, however, and into practical matters: As the son of a university administrator, I received a free college education, leaving me with no student debt – a rarity for an American university student. Because of my freedom from debt, I could pursue work with less attachment to financial remuneration. I yearned for exotic experiences that, stripped of comfort and convenience, would place me far outside my normal "comfort zone" requiring significant adaption to a new way of living. So I moved to Turkey, where I taught English for a year.

My spirit of unconventionality continued to burn, growing with every passing day, and consuming my time with a comprehensive self-study of all things entrepreneurial. From these many hours of rigorous research grew my first online business – TOEFL Speaking Teacher (TST) – a niche online English school focused on preparing foreign students for a difficult English entrance exam.

Through the medium of TST, I created enough financial independence to begin publicly speaking out about psychedelics while traveling the world.

Two realizations and a way forward

In July 2015, two friends visited me in Budapest. Both had previous experience with psychedelics, and were interested in the surging trend of microdosing. We began our time together with a microdose of LSD and a thorough exploration of the magnificent city of Budapest. After an excellent first experience, we chose to step-up our game and consume 250 micrograms in the foothills of the city.

Rising at 6:30 a.m., we consumed the LSD upon awakening, then called an Uber to drive us to Budapest's largest park, overlooking the Danube and the area's cascading hills. LSD normally takes about 45 minutes to kick in, and so, just as the "come-up" began, we settled into a beautiful meadow, with spectacular views of the city.

Delving into extensive conversation while under the influence, we came to a couple of profound realizations, which led to the creation of The Third Wave.

- Realization #1: psychedelics are valuable tools, and the future of psychedelic use will be less about "getting high" and more about tangible benefits in everyday life.

- Realization #2: with the growing resurgence of research in psychedelics, and the re-evaluation of cannabis as an illicit substance, more and more people were going to be interested in using psychedelic substances for personal benefit and growth. However, to make this really "catch on," the "hippie" vibe of the '60s needed to be stripped away and replaced by an aesthetic and brand with which mainstream culture could identify. In other words, psychedelics had a PR problem, and we wanted to fix it.

While still under the influence of psychedelics, we labeled this cultural movement "The Third Wave of Psychedelics," a creative play on the expression "Third Wave Coffee" (the movement that led to coffee being perceived more as an artisanal foodstuff than a mere commodity). When my close friend Nico came up with this name, I immediately said "yes" without an inkling as to *why* I liked it so much.

Then, after returning home in the evening, I double checked the legitimacy of such a name. Did it *actually* make sense to call this The Third Wave?

It did, in fact. The "First Wave" was indigenous use of psychedelic substances for thousands of years, including ayahuasca in the Amazon, soma in Ancient India, and kykeon in Ancient Greece.

The "Second Wave" was the countercultural movement of the 1960s, when these substances were re-introduced into the Western zeitgeist.

The "Third Wave" is a cultural movement made possible by a number of external forces, including the re-evaluation of cannabis, the growing body of medical research, and the renewed interest in tech and entrepreneurial circles. The Third Wave is less interested in the "experience" than in the tangible benefits one can incorporate *because* of the experience. To ensure the sustainability of such a push, we concentrated on psychedelic education and community building, draped in a distinctly curated aesthetic.

Microdosing takes over the media

Simultaneous to my psychedelic experiences, there was an explosion of media reports about microdosing. A November 2015 story in *Rolling Stone* magazine[iv] described the growing number of people in the Bay Area microdosing to improve their work performance. "The typical profile there is an "übersmart twentysomething" curious to see whether microdosing will help him or her work through technical problems and become more innovative," the piece states.

"Microdosing has helped me come up with some new designs to explore and new ways of thinking," the story's subject, a tech entrepreneur, claims. "You would be surprised at how many people are actually doing it. It's crazy awesome."

After the *Rolling Stone* story hit, numerous other publications followed up with their own dives into the world of microdosing. One of the most in-depth was published in *Wired* magazine[v] in August of 2016. The piece cites numerous residents of San Francisco and Silicon Valley who have joined the microdosing trend, noting that many are software engineers, biologists, and mathematicians.

"It helps me think more creatively and stay focused," a subject using the pseudonym Lily says in the article after she switched from using Adderall to microdosing psilocybin. "I manage my stress with ease and am able to keep my perspective healthy in a way that I was unable to before."

Another subject, a research chemist who goes by Joseph, calls microdosing psilocybin akin to "tuning a guitar."

Pharmacology professor David Nichols hypothesizes in the article that microdosing works as a stimulant by activating dopamine pathways and exciting the central cortex, similar to the effect of pills like Adderall and Ritalin but without addictive properties or other harmful side effects. Many of the young stars of Silicon Valley came from a university culture where they gobbled up prescription medications to help study, and continued to use them after graduation to gain an edge in the professional world. However, mood swings and withdrawal symptoms cause many to turn away from pills. Microdosing, proponents report, brings equal or better mental benefits, but in a gentler and healthier way.

"It makes me work in such a focused way," a software developer identified as Blake tells the magazine about microdosing with LSD. "It gets your brain out of its regular grooves and helps you snap out of unproductive trains of thought." Another described his mind as a supercomputer.

The popularity of microdosing stems from a culture of people trying to get the very most from their mental performance, the *Wired* article suggests. "We, in reality, enhance our brain functions through good sleep, exercise, nutrition, social interaction, coffee," neuroscientist and neurologist Dena Dubal is quoted, "and many continue to try and enhance brain function through new technologies and, in some cases, medications."

Where we stand now

My story, at this point, comes full circle to where we stand today: microdosing psychedelics for enhanced well-being and accelerated skill development. In accepting that influencers in the tech scene will build the future in which we'll live, what better avenue to mainstreaming psychedelics than curating a palatable, non-threatening message about their benefits.

I came to this conclusion by asking a few questions:

- How do we create a message about psychedelics that resonates with a mainstream crowd by stripping off the "hippie" vibe and present psychedelics as something "normal" folks do?
- How do we start building bridges with the most influential people in society, with an understanding that psychedelics and particularly microdosing can help us build a better world?
- Why has microdosing – an area of psychedelics without any clinical research – taken off in popularity?

Which leads to my own reason for microdosing.

Like many other men raised in American culture, particularly in a heavily Calvinist upbringing, all my external cultural signaling pointed toward the need to produce if I wanted to be valued. So, my entry point to microdosing stemmed from this desire: I wanted to microdose to be more effective to easily access flow states, and overcome procrastination and creative resistance.

But what I got from microdosing – presence, engagement, intimacy, flow states, leadership development, and more – transcended my initial desires. What I thought would be a nice little hack to overcome procrastination became a practice that completely transformed my approach to work, relationships, and, generally, life.

And now, I want to share why this beneficial practice may also transform yours.

---

iv

http://www.rollingstone.com/culture/features/how-lsd-microdosing-became-the-hot-new-business-trip-20151120

v

http://www.wired.co.uk/article/lsd-microdosing-drugs-silicon-valley

Chapter 2: The Story of Microdosing

The basic concept of microdosing is nothing new. Albert Hofmann, who first synthesized LSD in 1938, considered it one of the drug's most promising, and least researched, applications. He was among the first to realize its antidepressant and cognition-enhancing potential,[vi] famously taking between 10 and 20 µg himself, twice a week, for the last few decades of his life.[vii]

Apparently he wasn't alone. As psychologist, author, and pioneer psychedelic researcher James Fadiman, Ph.D., later found out, others have been microdosing for decades. Indeed, various indigenous groups have taken microdoses of psychedelic plants for hundreds, even thousands of years. And Terence McKenna went so far as to credit our evolution as *Homo sapiens* to *Homo erectus'* micro-consumption of psilocybin mushrooms while pack hunting.[viii]

Having already studied the creativity- and concentration-boosting effects of LSD and mescaline (at moderate doses) during the 1960s, Fadiman readily accepted the testimony of Robert Forte and others who gained similar benefits from microdoses. Intrigued, in 2008 he put together a self-study protocol with clinical psychologist Sophia Korb, Ph.D. and began soliciting reports from users, hoping to map out this uncharted area of psychedelic experience.

With the publication of *The Psychedelic Explorer's Guide* in 2011, Fadiman formally introduced the term "microdosing" to the psychedelic lexicon. Packed with anecdotal reports and breakthrough transformations, as well as practical tips on how to repeat them, his book inspired countless others to experiment for themselves. Hundreds of people requested Fadiman's protocol, and many returned reports – not only on LSD and psilocybin, but also ayahuasca, iboga, and other, more obscure substances like Syrian rue.

In 2014, the r/microdosing subreddit was set up as a place for microdosers to share their experiences. Since then, it has become an extremely active forum with tens of thousands of subscribers and a steady stream of new members.

In March 2015, Fadiman appeared on the massively popular *Tim Ferriss Show* podcast. With its wide and relatively mainstream appeal – covering business, "biohacking," personal development, exercise, and spirituality, among other topics – the podcast marked a turning point in the microdosing movement. No longer the exclusive domain of the psychedelic fringe, now some of the most influential people in the world, including venture capitalists and tech entrepreneurs, were in on it.

As others reported the trend, they only encouraged its growth. The initial wave of media coverage focused primarily on microdosing for productivity among high-powered professionals and Silicon Valley types.

However, not all of the coverage was complimentary. An article in *Forbes* published shortly after the November 2015 *Rolling Stone* piece criticized the very concept of microdosing.[ix] Unfortunately, the author had little in the way of new insight, instead leaning on old stereotypes and propaganda to label LSD use as categorically dangerous and a "disturbing trend" while dismissing even the possibility of beneficial results.

The *Forbes* piece was in the minority, however. Most of the coverage of microdosing was open to the idea that there might be something to the wave of successful engineers and entrepreneurs touting their use of psychedelics.

A *GQ* story claimed, "micro-dosing had made [the subject's] thinking clearer, allowing him to make 'better connections between his thoughts and words.' The difference was manifest in the way he wrote. With a micro-dose of LSD, he felt abnormally productive, quick, and clever in e-mails.[x]"

In Portland, thousands of people are microdosing with LSD or psilocybin, an article in *Willamette Week* suggests.[xi] "We've had dentists and doctors, professional musicians, students, of course, and everyday regular lower-wage [workers]," a woman named Helen says of a new psychedelic research and exploration group. "Really, I don't see any kind of trend in terms of profession."

Many microdosing enthusiasts have congregated on Reddit, participating in a group that had more than 17,500 subscribers as of the summer of 2017.[xii] People on the forum discuss all aspects of microdosing, from dosage to different substances to the results that they found. A poster who took microdoses of psilocybin for seven weeks, for example, reported results similar to the accounts showing up in news stories. "My focusing on work ability increased dramatically (and has been almost since the beginning)," the poster wrote. "My work mood has improved too. i keep brief notes about how i feel, from grumpy to meh to good, and almost every day is good."[xiii]

On another post, users talked about how microdosing did (or did not) help them solve math problems. "I do very abstract maths daily (I'm in academia), and for me, micro-dosing seems to help with the creative problem solving aspect, but makes me slightly worse at tedious calculations/brute-force proofs," a poster wrote.

"I'm in engineering," another added, "and it really helps me tackle a problem in creative ways if I find old methods don't work."[xiv]

The majority of reports – at least on the internet – fell somewhere between cautiously optimistic and eagerly instructive. Those criticizing the trend were either ill informed or sensationalistic – In other words, business as usual for the "Just Say No" camp. The *Forbes* article, for instance, refused to admit even the possibility of beneficial results, while The *Daily Mail* insisted that the "LSD 'microdosing' trend can put your life at risk"[xv] without any supporting evidence.

Meanwhile, Fadiman's Phase I research was published in *Psychedelic Press, Volume XV*, along with a list of conditions that people had successfully treated with microdosing.

The January 2017 publication of Ayelet Waldman's, *A Really Good Day: How Microdosing Made a Mega Difference in My Mood, My Marriage, and My Life* further catalysed the spread of microdosing's appeal, this time from the relatively niche biohacking crowd to the realm of the stay-at-home mom. Crucially, Waldman reframed microdosing as a tool for mental health – not merely a billionaire's plaything. Within the wider context of mainstream medical marijuana and the FDA's designation of MDMA and ketamine as "breakthrough therapies," it was an idea whose time had come.

Accordingly, the second wave of media coverage focused more on the therapeutic applications of microdosing, and of psychedelics in general.

A piece in *The New Yorker*[xvi] profiled Waldman as a productive, middle-class wife and mother who, having tried many other treatments without success, finally turned to LSD as a way of saving her relationship with her family. The article also highlighted the safety of LSD, almost without reservation, and practically lamented its illegality. Other reports – in *Mashable,*[xvii] *The Economist,*[xviii] *Huffington Post,*[xix] *Crave,*[xx] *Willamette Week,*[xxi] and the BBC,[xxii] among many others – took a similarly sympathetic approach to microdosing and the people who do it.

Perhaps unsurprisingly, we're now beginning to see the early stirrings of serious microdosing research by major institutions. The Beckley Foundation and Imperial College London, for example, have crowdfunded a brain-imaging study to measure pattern recognition and creativity on microdoses of LSD.[xxiii] The Australian Research Council's Centre of Excellence in Cognition and Its Disorders (ARC CCD) carried out an online survey of microdosers, paid for by the Australian government.[xxiv] Other institutions, including MAPS, UCL, NYU, and Johns Hopkins, have continued to research the wider utility of psychedelics at higher doses. According to Fadiman, double-blind microdosing studies using placebos could eventually pave the way for FDA approval.[xxv]

Meanwhile, microdosing has become almost normalized in the media, and the coverage necessarily more nuanced and engaged. *Rolling Stone's* September 2017 piece,[xxvi] for instance, took a closer look at my one-to-one coaching services, barely mentioning the controversy and novelty of microdosing itself – the media's earlier preoccupation.

When I started The Third Wave, I knew microdosing would be key to legitimizing psychedelics. Now, with the genie well and truly out of the bottle, it falls to us – each one of us – to keep spreading the word. As consciousness researcher David Jay Brown urged in *The New Science of Psychedelics*: "If we learn how to improve our lives with psychedelics ... it's our responsibility, our sacred duty, to share what we've learned with the rest of the world."[xxvii]

vi

Michael Horowtiz, "An Interview with Albert Hofmann," High Times, July, 1976, https://erowid.org/culture/characters/hofmann_albert/hofmann_albert_interview1.pdf

vii

"FAQ on Microdosing," microdosingpsychedelics.com, accessed October 4, 2017, https://sites.google.com/view/microdosingpsychedelics/faq-on-microdosing

viii

Terence McKenna, Food of the Gods: The Search for the Original Tree of Knowledge – A Radical History of Plants, Drugs, and Human Evolution (New York: Bantam, 1992)

ix

https://www.forbes.com/sites/robertglatter/2015/11/27/lsd-microdosing-the-new-job-enhancer-in-silicon-valley-and-beyond/2/#4e3dba902c9f

x

http://www.gq.com/story/micro-dosing-lsd

xi

http://www.wweek.com/culture/2017/04/18/can-lsd-make-you-better-at-your-job-the-guy-in-the-cubicle-next-to-you-might-be-trying-it/

xii

https://www.reddit.com/r/microdosing/

xiii

https://www.reddit.com/r/microdosing/comments/68fnr0/random_observations_7_weeks_in_md_mushrooms/
xiv

https://www.reddit.com/r/microdosing/comments/67ctik/microdosing_and_mathematics/
xv

"LSD 'microdosing' trend popular with tech entrepreneurs may be putting their lives at risk, claim

Cambridge University scientists," Daily Mail Online, February 17, 2017, http://www.dailymail.co.uk/sciencetech/article-4231488/Does-taking-LSD-work-REALLY-boost-productivity.html
xvi

20 Nathan Heller, "How Ayelet Waldman Found a Calmer Life on Tiny Doses of LSD," New Yorker, January 12, 2017, https://www.newyorker.com/culture/persons-of-interest/how-ayelet-waldman-found-a-calmer-life-on-tiny-doses-of-lsd
xvii

Maria Gallucci, "Researchers want to know the effects of taking small doses of LSD to self-medicate," Mashable, May 9, 2017, http://mashable.com/2017/05/09/lsd-microdosing-scientific-study/
xviii

Emma Hogan, "Turn On, Tune In, Drop By the Office," The Economist 1843, August/September, 2017, https://www.1843magazine.com/features/turn-on-tune-in-drop-by-the-office
xix

Craig K. Comstock, "Psychedelics and Normality," Huffpost, July 25, 2017, http://www.huffingtonpost.com/entry/psychedelics-and-normality_us_5977a1dae4b01cf1c4bb73dc
xx

Miss Rosen, "Better Living Through Microdosing," Crave Online, May 5, 2017, http://www.craveonline.com/culture/1258901-better-living-microdosing
xxi

Matthew Korfhage, "We're Entering A New Golden Age of Psychedelics, and Portland is Leading the Way," Willamette Week, April 18, 2017, http://www.wweek.com/culture/2017/04/18/can-lsd-make-you-better-at-your-job-the-guy-in-the-cubicle-next-to-you-might-be-trying-it/
xxii

Catrin Nye, "Microdosing: The people taking LSD with their breakfast," BBC News, April 10, 2017, http://www.bbc.co.uk/news/health-39516345
xxiii

"Support Our LSD Microdosing Study," Beckley Foundation, accessed October 4, 2017, http://beckleyfoundation.org/microdosing-lsd/
xxiv

"Microdosing Study: Are You Experienced or Interested in "Microdosing"?" MAPS, accessed October 4, 2017, https://www.maps.org/research/articles/133-participate-in-research-2/auxiliary-studies-not-sponsored-by-maps/6344-microdosing-study-are-you-experienced-or-interested-in-microdosing

26

xxv

Jason Koebler, "A Brief History of Microdosing," Motherboard, November 24, 2015, https://motherboard.vice.com/en_us/article/gv5p5y/a-brief-history-of-microdosing

xxvi

Stephie Grob Plante, "Meet the World's First Online LSD Microdosing Coach," Rolling Stone, September 7, 2017, http://www.rollingstone.com/culture/features/meet-the-worlds-first-online-lsd-microdosing-coach-w499104

xxvii

David Jay Brown, The New Science of Psychedelics: At the Nexus of Culture, Consciousness, and Spirituality (Vermont: Park Street Press, 2013)

Chapter 3: What Do People Experience From Microdosing?

Microdosing involves consuming sub-perceptual doses of psychedelics – most commonly LSD and psilocybin – in a fixed protocol, like two times per week. Unlike "macro-dosing," microdosing is intended to integrate your psychedelic consumption into your daily routine to boost creativity, improve energy, increase mental focus, and enjoy better interpersonal relations.

By no means are you guaranteed to experience all, or indeed any, of these effects. But the sheer number and depth of the benefits ascribed to microdosing are astounding, and certainly worth outlining. In fact, they seem to cover the whole gamut of human experience, from the minutiae of everyday life to grand philosophical insights.

The effects of microdosing have been well publicized – not least by us at The Third Wave. So when we surveyed participants in our microdosing course about their motivations, we were not surprised by the wide-ranging scope of their answers. Evenly spread between the ages of 18 and 75, the majority of participants hoped that microdosing could help them with at least one of the following:

- Professional development
- Finding purpose
- Increasing energy, focus, and motivation, or overcoming procrastination
- Enhancing or reawakening creativity
- Opening up to others and improving relationships
- Nurturing self-acceptance
- Finding general contentedness
- Letting go of bad habits
- Overcoming fears
- Attaining self-realization
- Improving mental health

– Optimizing athletic performance

Many were simply curious to see what microdosing could do for them, or what it would feel like, having been intrigued by the positive media coverage.

My own initial expectations ran parallel to some of those listed above, and, as I mentioned in Chapter 1, were firmly rooted in my Calvinist, middle-class American upbringing. Specifically, I wanted to become more productive. I wanted to stop procrastinating and grow my online teaching business. To me, microdosing was a "life hack" worth trying.

Like so many others, however, what I actually gained was far more useful, and more transformative, than I'd hoped for. Among the benefits I experienced were an end to my social anxiety and insecurities, the ability to overcome creative blocks, better empathy and compassion, more engagement in my relationships, and a sense of presence or mindfulness that I'd rarely felt before. Unexpectedly, microdosing also shed light on points of vulnerability that I didn't even know were there.

As for productivity, not only was I able to grow my online English teaching business – thanks to a much improved ability to handle complex tasks and integrate new information – I also launched a second: The Third Wave.

Others have experienced similar boosts to their professional development through microdosing. "I feel deeply connected to my work, focused and in the flow," wrote "Madeline," one of researcher and author James Fadiman's earliest survey respondents.[xxviii] One of our own forum members also reported being able to maintain focus "for longer and with higher intensity" when microdosing, while remaining "open and mindful" to colleagues.[xxix] Another forum member, microdosing with psilocybin truffles, found that work just flowed. He was able to see what needed to be done and do it before moving on to the next thing.[xxx]

Entrepreneur Janet Chang, speaking on The Third Wave Podcast, found her productivity to be measurably improved only in specific areas, like sales and outreach.[xxi] However, she experienced vast improvements in a number of other areas, including emotional self-awareness, mood, creativity, and sociability. In fact, Janet did such an exemplary job at self-tracking throughout her year-long experiment with microdosing psilocybin that it's worth taking a closer look.

Careful to guard against the placebo effect by avoiding others' accounts of their experiences, she tried to be as objective as possible, experimenting with various dosage levels and keeping detailed reports on a number of key data points. These included the quantity and nature of her thoughts, her creativity, and her sociability. She also used rankings between 1 and 5 to rate her anxiety, mood, and productivity levels, and categorized the numbers as follows:

1: extremely low
2: slightly lower than normal
3: normal (baseline)
4: slightly higher than normal
5: extremely high

At 0.15-0.2 grams of psilocybin mushrooms, (Fadiman's suggested microdose) she experienced mild improvements to her mood and anxiety levels (rated 3.25 and 2.13, respectively) but not to her productivity (which idled at 2.75).

The next dosage level was 0.2-0.4 g, which she had the opportunity to test between two different work environments—one less orderly and more social, and the other more organized and mostly independent. In the former environment, she found she was extremely productive (4.71) but also highly anxious (3.43). In the latter, she was somewhat less anxious (3.17) but also less focused (2.61). Her mood was exaggerated in general, characterized by higher highs and lower lows.

Finally, at 0.5 g, which is typically described as a "minidose" or "creative dose," Janet was surprised to find her anxiety levels almost negligible at 1.41

and her mood and productivity levels significantly improved at 4.50 and 4.07, respectively.[xxxii]

Sub-perceptual sparkle

For many, microdoses transform work into a kind of "creative play," as "Madeline" put it, or "professional satori" – a state in which "you are doing what you do professionally, you are doing it well, time passes quickly, and you are pleased with your output."[xxxiii]

That said, it's important to note that microdosing doesn't seem reliably useful for getting through work you'd rather not be doing. It simply adds what Third Wave contributor Rosalind Stone describes as a "sub-perceptual sparkle."[xxxiv]

Certainly this accords with my own experience of microdosing and the way in which it helped to accelerate my progress along the path I was already on, the path that I knew to be right for me. What microdosing isn't, and what it shouldn't be seen as, is a way to make the wrong path less arduous. In fact, far from bypassing these resistances, it can actually be helpful in identifying them and making the necessary changes.

Microdosing also facilitated my own leadership development – another key area of professional development for some. We'll look at this in more detail in Chapter 11, but it's interesting to note how leadership can benefit from microdosing. Leadership straddles the boundary between professional and personal development, drawing on openness, receptivity, engagement, trust, empathy, and compassion – all of which may be developed through microdosing. "Madeline" found her skills as a listener greatly improved and her friends and family felt "truly seen" in conversations with her. Indeed, several family members trusted her so much after she'd started microdosing that they appointed her executor of their estates.[xxxv]

Mindfulness and self-reflection, that is, awareness of our personal motivations and emotions, also underpin good leadership. Again, these are qualities enhanced by microdosing. Rosalind Stone, for instance, hadn't even been aware she was depressed until she started. And others find themselves dealing with surprising emotions that lay hidden beneath the surface.

That's not to say microdosing causes you to live "inside your head." On the contrary, many users find they're more present and better able to respond to the demands of the moment. As one of our survey respondents put it, "microdosing doesn't allow me to be anywhere but in the present moment... I am incapable of worrying about what's going to happen next week, tomorrow, or even five minutes from now."

As such, microdosers tend to be less critical – about themselves and their situation – and generally more content. "What I find is that it's easy for me to appreciate everyone and everything in my life, to easily and naturally step into a space of gratitude and sustain it," said one of Fadiman's sources. A Third Wave forum poster was more specific, recalling how a pizza he'd ordered many times before somehow tasted like the best he'd had in years after microdosing, giving him a "blissful and grateful feeling."[xxxvi]

Obviously, this has implications for mental health, and many turn to microdosing for anxiety, depression, PTSD, OCD, ADD/ADHD, and a range of other conditions, as well as for weaning off conventional medications.

(Note: If you plan to go off your medications, it is best to do so under the supervision of a physician.)

Depression and anxiety

By now, the ability of psychedelics such as LSD, psilocybin, and others – at a full dose – to help treat and alleviate mental disorders such as depression and anxiety is well-established. Numerous studies have suggested that these substances can help people confront and move past their suffering, even when conventional methods of treatment and pharmaceutical interventions such as selective serotonin reuptake inhibitors (SSRIs) have failed.

More research is currently underway to advance our understanding of exactly how psychedelics help people handle these and other similar mental disorders. Many subjects report that their experiences using these substances helped them grapple with the root causes of their disorders with new perspective and clarity, along with bringing a renewed sense of gratitude and connection with the world.

While the research on microdosing is far less robust than the body of work on full-dose psychedelics, an abundance of anecdotal evidence suggests that it may have similar long-term effects as large amounts of psilocybin or LSD.

Indeed, a number of Third Wave readers reported that they decided to try microdosing specifically because they wanted a new avenue to help mitigate depression and anxiety-related issues.

"At the very beginning of microdosing (on LSD), I was struggling with some anxiety and depression revolving around sexual trauma and fully coming into myself as a queer woman," one reader wrote.

"I have a history of anxiety/depression and have found in the past that these symptoms have been more controlled in times that I had experimented with psychedelics," another reported. "I had heard about microdosing in the last year or so and thought it would be a logical experiment."

"I found that conventional medicine [for anxiety and depression] was not working and the side effects were bad," said one respondent.

Many readers were successful in their attempts to treat certain mental disorders. Out of 51 responses to one survey, 60.8 percent said that microdosing helped with depression, 31.4 percent found relief from general anxiety, and 25.5 percent said that it helped with social anxiety.

On a second survey, 229 respondents gave microdosing an average score of 3.8 on a scale of 1 to 6 for lowering anxiety, and 4.1 for lowering depression. "Only thing that helped my depression, it's a miracle medicine!!" one reader wrote in. "I have fought depression for some 6-7 years since adolescence, micro-dosing has, so far, consistently helped me get on with my day to day, just as much on no MD days as MD days. This also applies to Social & general Anxiety which has been less severe but experienced for the same period," another reported.

"Sometimes I feel myself as free, open and independent as when I was kid and had good times. A feeling that I was looking for really long," an individual said to The Third Wave.

Fadiman writes that improved mental health, in general, was a common result experienced by microdosers. "It appears that behavior changes were real, observable, and pervasive and that most changes were improvements that reflected increased self-worth, reduced anxiety, and lessened feelings of inadequacy," he wrote in his book, *The Psychedelic Explorer's Guide.* "In addition, the subjects formed deeper and more meaningful relationships."[xxxvii]

Fadiman and his co-researcher Sophia Korb presented some of the preliminary results of a new study on microdosing at Psychedelic Science 2017, a gathering sponsored by the Multidisciplinary Association for Psychedelic Studies (MAPS). "The largest group of people who write us are people with depression and treatment-resistant depression," he said to an audience assembled to hear him speak. Out of an initial 418 respondents, 35 percent cited depression as the reason they began microdosing and 27 percent cited anxiety, while 58 percent said they were motivated by a combination of both depression and anxiety.[xxxviii]

In a survey Fadiman conducted, respondents reported that after microdosing they experienced an overall increase in feelings of determination, activity, alertness, strength, and enthusiasm, with a decrease in feelings of depression, disturbance, guilt, and fear. The results also produced some preliminary evidence that microdosing could be helpful for people with PTSD and bipolar disorder; however, the research team wasn't comfortable making a definitive determination without gathering more information first.

Fadiman's research partner Sophia Korb presented quotes from people with treatment-resistant depression who found microdosing helpful. "I have noticed that my 'mental chatter' is considerably less than it was prior to this study," one respondent wrote. "I'm feeling very focused, very energetic, very alert," another said. One participant said "My self talk feels like from a third person view."

On the flip side, some people who said they were trying to treat anxiety reported to Fadiman that microdosing increased, not decreased, their anxious feelings. In that same vein, a Third Wave reader reported that microdosing actually heightened anxiety "when combined with excessive caffeine." Another reader wrote in: "Can enhance paranoia, be careful."

Yet, other Third Wave readers have praised microdosing for its effect on both depression and anxiety: "I overcame my depression with microdosing because I can consistently be productive and happy with it as a creative booster," the reader wrote. "It also eliminates any anxiety I get because I never used to raise my hand in class. I smoke a lot of cannabis and it's unhealthy to overindulge. I found microdosing to make me feel the need to be productive so I smoke much less when I microdose and don't indulge just to smoke."

Another respondent had a similar experience: "Happiness and sense of gratitude was pervasive and extended into personal life creating a quiet sense of well being – anti-depression. General anxiety and stress decreased for the most part."

"I can function without anxiety for the first time in years," a survey participant said to The Third Wave. "I feel that my attention span is greater, I'm concentrating like never before. When I was suffering with pain I was given a lot of prescription pain pills and was quickly becoming addicted to them. Microdosing instantly helped me stop taking the several pills a day I was taking just so I could get out of bed, and I haven't touched them since."

The ability to get a handle on depression and anxiety and reduce or eliminate reliance on pharmaceutical pills is a key component to the promise of psychedelics, since they do not carry the same side effects of SSRIs and other commonly prescribed medicines, such as insomnia, drowsiness and problems with sexual function. Indeed, despite the ostensible comfort that receiving a diagnosis and prescription from a licensed psychiatrist might bring, we don't really have a thorough understanding of how SSRIs work or when they can be most effectively deployed. For one thing, we don't know what the proper level of serotonin should be for any given person, nor do we have a way of measuring it.[xxxix] A recent study found that many psychiatrists essentially take a shotgun approach to their practice, putting patients on a number of pills at once in hope that one of them, or some combination, is able to help.[xl] Another study found that certain SSRIs such as Paxil and Prozac had the same effect on depression as giving patients a sugar pill; in other words, they failed to outperform a placebo.[xli] In antidepressant clinical trials conducted by Massachusetts General Hospital and Harvard Medical School, 30 to 40 percent of the subjects responded positively to a placebo.[xlii]

In the book *Anatomy of an Epidemic*, author Robert Whitaker suggests that our pharmaceutical-first regime of treating mental disorders not only fails to help people recover over the long-term, it actually increases the chances that people will become dependent on drugs. Even as the prescription of pills has skyrocketed, the number of people diagnosed with disabling psychiatric problems has also gone through the roof – from 355,000 in 1955 to over 4 million as of 2007, Whitaker writes.[xliii]

But while pharmaceutical pills do help alleviate symptoms of anxiety and depression for some, microdosing appears to help people attack the root cause of their problems.

The key to the power of psychedelics, many reports assert, is improved self awareness. One respondent to a Third Wave survey took a stab at explaining why feelings of anxiety decreased after microdosing: "I became much more self aware and willing to look at my shortcomings and character defects in a non judgmental way. Example: I noticed that when I couldn't control a situation that I would get very anxious. An hour later as I was observing my mental focus on this, and some physical reactions to this, I began to have a dialogue with myself to understand why this was happening. I realized that it is completely human to want to be in control of everything. I told myself that the beauty in this is that I am not in control of what goes on around me and this was a big relief. I also noticed that it took a little time to start noticing these things fully. This was a **JOURNEY** with curves and a lot of learning about myself which I am grateful for."

Accounts in popular media have also supported the notion of microdosing helping people with anxiety and depression. In the 2015 *Rolling Stone* piece that kicked off the wave of reporting on microdosing, Jim Fadiman cited the positive results. "His correspondents have told him regular microdosing has alleviated a bevy of disorders, including depression, migraines and chronic-fatigue syndrome, while increasing outside-the-box thinking," the article states.[xliv]

In the in-depth *Wired* story mentioned before, Lily mentioned more good tidings. "I have the physical wellness bit down but the mental wellness is something I've struggled with. Microdosing helps manage my anxiety both in the short and long term."[xlv]

The article in Portland's *Willamette Week* I wrote about in Chapter 2 describes a middle-aged mother and musician. "She suffered from anxiety and PTSD from childhood trauma that was so severe she could no longer perform," the story says, "but taking low-dose mushrooms gave her the fortitude to get back onstage."[xlvi]

In fact, reports from other publications and our surveys of Third Wave readers find mental health issues – primarily depression – flourishing among people putting in impossibly long hours in a high-stakes environment where most startups fail to become sustainable businesses. The pressure cooker conditions are combined with a stigma for showing any sign of perceived weakness that could jeopardize funding from investors who might view mental health issues as a risky variable. Nearly half the entrepreneurs who responded to one particular survey reported some type of mental health condition.[xlvii]

In some cases, neural atypicalities that help coders come up with innovative solutions and display unflagging endurance also weigh heavily on their mental health. "Many of the personality traits found in entrepreneurs – creativity, extroversion, open mindedness and a propensity for risk are also traits associated with ADHD, bipolar spectrum conditions, depression and substance abuse," notes a CNN story about the suicide of Eric Salvatierra, a former executive at eBay, PayPal, and Skype.[xlviii]

In addition to its benefits toward creativity and problem solving, one reason microdosing might be so prevalent in Silicon Valley is because it allows hard-working professionals to manage struggles with depression in a healthier and more productive manner.

Of course, the practice isn't limited to only Silicon Valley workers. As I mentioned in the last chapter, by far the biggest splash in the public consciousness regarding microdosing as a tool to battle mental disorders came when author Ayelet Waldman published *A Really Good Day: How Microdosing Made a Mega Difference in My Mood, My Marriage, and My Life.*[xlix] The 2017 book speaks of how Waldman was losing control of her moods and alienating her family, until she found relief through microdosing LSD.

"I believe that these drugs have great therapeutic potential," Waldman said during a podcast interview with The Third Wave. "This month changed my life, and I am sad every day that I can't keep doing it legally."[l]

Instantly, Waldman's work was highlighted across the mediasphere. "Countless prescription pharmaceuticals had failed to stabilize her chronic mood disorders, including depression and Bipolar II disorder, and, more recently, her premenstrual dysphoric disorder, a particularly disabling form of premenstrual syndrome," the *New York Times* wrote about her journey. "Her tempestuous psyche, she said, was tearing apart her marriage and raising thoughts of suicide."[li]

"I would have blown up my marriage," she told the newspaper. "I had blown up my marriage. I would have left [her husband] Michael to punish myself. And that's so crazy. All he ever did was love me, and try, but when you love someone who is mentally ill, you're just pouring water into a bucket with a hole in it. It can be exhausting. I think the microdosing actually sealed the hole. Now it's a smaller hole, but we all have to keep on pouring water."

She went into more detail in an interview with the *Guardian.* "Within the first couple of doses, it was like the computer of my brain had been restarted," she said. "I was still moody. I had some really good days, but there were also crappy days, and days when it was just the normal shit. Somehow, though, the bad days were not hellish days, and so I had the capacity to work on issues I just couldn't before. Sure, I was hoping for joy. What I got instead was enough distance from the pain I was in to work on the things that were causing it."[lii]

"The horrible crippling depression that I entered the experiment with – that was gone," Waldman said on the *Today Show.* "It allowed me to kind of reset my brain and emotions."[liii]

With Waldman as its avatar, the notion of microdosing became more widespread and popular than ever, and more people became exposed to its potential. "The mood improvement that coincided with her microdosing changed her whole view of depression," the *New Yorker* weighed in. "It was almost the first time in my life I had perspective on what my moods are," she said to the magazine. "Now, when I slip back into the bad feelings, I know it could get better overnight. And also: there is better."[liv]

In a powerful statement, a Third Wave reader shared a similar anecdote about a life-saving experiment with microdosing: "Immediately I felt less anxiety. The little things I worried about on a day to day basis, didn't worry me anymore. I was able to recognize how "little" they actually were for the first time ever. I felt more connected to the universe and experienced an overwhelming amount of peace. I was in a lot of pain at the time I tried microdosing. I was taking an obscene amount of pain pills and I knew it was only a matter of time before I would have to try something stronger and it scared me. The first time I microdosed I felt like I wasn't going to die anymore. For several weeks leading up to me microdosing I was convinced that whatever I was experiencing was going to kill me. After the mushrooms kicked in for the very first time I wasn't afraid of dying anymore. I believed that no matter what was going to happen that I was going to be ok. Microdosing saved my life."

From addiction to exertion

Sometimes good mental health comes down to deconditioning ourselves or letting go of negative thought patterns and behaviors. Addiction is an obvious example, and some have been able to manage it through microdosing. One Reddit user, for instance, found they were suddenly able to "mindfully and joyfully accomplish tasks" they'd otherwise have drunk alcohol for.[lv] Others have found their cravings substantially diminished.

Some people have been able to manage even physical issues through microdosing, including chronic pain, migraines, and menstrual cramps. This relief has been known to outlast the protocol itself.[lvi]

More commonly, people report a general feeling of health and wellness, often rooted in a stronger mind-body connection. Many microdosers have remarked on this. One, mentioned in a 2017 *Economist* article, felt "sharper, more aware of what [the] body needs" on 1P-LSD,[lvii] while Fadiman's respondent, "Madeline" felt "so healthy and connected to [her] body" that she began to cry.

Needless to say, this is of particular utility in sports and other physical activities, including yoga, martial arts, and dance. One Reddit user – a professional dancer – reported improvements to balance, stamina, and energy, along with a far greater sense of interconnectivity between the muscles.[lviii] Others have reported stamina boosts for cycling, running, and other exercises.[lix-lx] "Within an hour after I swallow my [microdose], I start feeling more energy," wrote one of Fadiman's sources, "It's a kind of bubbling burning on a very low level; my cells and systems are pumped up with a noticeable kind of buzz...What's lovely is that it's a kind of good secondary energy, that is, I can use it to work out with weights, do Pilates, ride my bike, or really just enjoy being with my body." Another source, having microdosed psilocybin for surfing, said, "I was so much more in my body and could feel deeper into it. I sensed the wave had come thousands of miles and that we were coming together for its last few seconds before it hit the beach. But what was best was feeling like I connected back into the greater world."[lxi]

That sense of presence and unity is of course beneficial for creativity as well, which we'll look at in Chapter 10, but also for self-realization. In *The Psychedelic Explorer's Guide*, "Charles" recounts becoming aware of the oneness inherent in the world: "What I feel that micro-dosing does is to slightly rearrange my neural furniture so that glimmers of full-on psychedelic states are constantly pouring into my awareness. I can see how the spider, her web, the wall the web is on, the house the wall is part of, the town the house is part of, and so on, are all connected. It becomes easy to see those connections, in fact, practically self-evident. And from there it's just a short step to radically affirming the rightness of the spider's web, just the way it is in this moment." "Anita" agreed, finding herself "more able to see the world as interrelated rather than disjointed" on microdoses of psilocybin.

What are your intentions?

So far, this chapter has covered the effects of microdosing on mental health, wellness, personal development, and creativity. At the Third Wave, we believe that whoever you are, your own intentions around microdosing will be critical to your experience.

Beginning a microdosing regimen is no casual decision. You're starting on an excursion that could offer profound benefits that endure for the rest of your life, whether you continue microdosing or not. One critical step to ensuring you get the most from your microdosing experience is to set your intentions before you start.

Intention is a key concept in psychedelic practices. An intention is a conscious aim, chosen based on your deeply held values, tied to an embodied action in the future. Your intention fuels the motivation to actually take action when the context is right, or to prevent an action from happening when the context is wrong.

Because psychedelic substances decrease order and increase volatility, a strong goal is necessary to offset distractions and stay on purpose. Without knowing where we are going, we are more likely to end up at a place we don't want to be. If we have a clear intention, however, we will discover the right opportunities to take the steps in the direction we aimed for. That's especially important when microdosing, where we want to integrate the beneficial properties of psychedelics into the context of our day-to-day lives.

Before you embark on your microdosing journey, consider taking the following steps:

1. Figure out your values

Good daily intentions set your focus around your personal values and as such are inspirational and motivating. First, however, you have to know what you value and where you're headed. Take a moment prior to diving directly into intention-setting to understand your unique perspective in the world. This experience is all about you, not in an egoic way, but as a means of bringing your best self to the forefront. Focus on bettering yourself in comparison to previous iterations of yourself.

For example, here are a few of my personal values:

- Conscious relationship matters most: That includes my relationship with myself, with my loved ones, with the earth and with my work.

- Experience over accumulation: Excess is to be avoided – excess consumption of material items, excess food, excess financial resources.

- Make the most of it: Life is a gift and I only have one opportunity (as far as I know). For that reason, I live with courage and always act from a place that aligns with who I am and what I want out of life.

2. Take inventory

To clarify your goals for your microdosing regimen, take inventory of what changes you'd like to make in your life, focusing on the upcoming month. Sit for a few minutes to consider each question, and write down an honest answer that comes from your heart, without censoring yourself. Don't worry about what you're supposed to want, or what others might think. The goal is to get closer to what really matters to you. As part of this process, consider visualizing your future self, having integrated these changes in your life.

- If you could choose only one thing that you could do better next month, what would it be?
- What would you like to learn more about in the next month?
- What habits would you like to improve?
    - At work or school?
    - With friends and family?
    - For health?
- What type of connections would you like to make with others?
- What worthwhile and personally meaningful leisure activities would you like to pursue?
- How could you improve your relationship with your partner(s), parents, children, and/or siblings?
- What would you like to have achieved a month from now, career wise?
- Are there specific areas in your life where you would like to gain more insight or wisdom?
- Think of someone who you admire. What qualities and virtues do they possess that you can integrate into your own life?
- What steps could you take to create a month of successfully growing towards your ideal self?
- Now, spend some time thinking about the outcome if you fail to pursue your goals and let your bad habits get out of control. What decisions would lead to a future you want to avoid?

3. Clarify and refine

Once you've figured out what you stand for, and how you would like the upcoming month to unfold, you need to translate your values into practical steps. The most powerful intentions follow an "if-then" structure, also called implementation intentions. The "if" refers to a specific moment in the future you want to be reminded of your value to inform your actions.

A few examples:

o "If I get distracted from my project, then I think of why I want to complete it, and return my focus back to the task at hand."

o "If I feel emotionally overwhelmed, then I take a moment to breathe in and remind myself to allow any feeling to arise."

o "If I see myself judging my creative output, then I keep going because I know it doesn't need to be perfect."

Always frame your intentions in the positive. "I want to trust myself" is better than "I want to stop being shy." Your aims should point to embodying some specific set of behaviors, so when you state your intention, you know what achieving your day's goal would actually look and feel like.

4. Set your intention and embark on your journey

It's helpful to set intentions for your microdosing journey as a whole, as well as how you would like each day to unfold. Declare. Write. Speak. Record. Internalize. Then hold yourself accountable for whether you're carrying out your desired actions. The day's intention should be something that you come back to often in your thoughts and that can help guide your decisions and behavior throughout the day. You might be amazed at how smoothly you progress toward your goals.

You also might find that your outcomes aren't exactly what you envisioned, or you change your mind about how to achieve what you want, but if you approach the process with integrity and honest self-reflection you will experience positive self-growth regardless and make a profound impact in your life for the better.

Now that you've assessed your values, inventoried your goals, and set your intention, keep in kind that the benefits of microdosing may outlast the protocol itself. It's not uncommon for the effects to be as pronounced, or more so, the day after microdosing or even the day after that. Some may find the lessons learned or skills developed stay with them indefinitely.

Naturally, not all experiences are positive and even the benefits can have downsides, which we'll look at in the next chapter. But the anecdotal evidence alone makes it abundantly clear how much more there is to microdosing than the "mere placebo" theory allows.

---

xxviii

James Fadiman, The Psychedelic Explorer's Guide: Safe, Therapeutic, and Sacred Journeys (Rochester, VT: Park Street Press, 2011)

xxix

Ivo Fugers, "Energy level increase/decrease," Third Wave forum post, April 29, 2017, https://forum.thethirdwave.co/threads/energy-level-increase-decrease.54/

xxx

tartalo, "Magic Truffle MD," Third Wave forum post, March 15, 2017, https://forum.thethirdwave.co/threads/magic-truffle-md.16/

xxxi

The Third Wave, "An Entrepreneur's Year-long Microdosing Experiment - with Janet Chang," podcast, https://thethirdwave.co/janet-chang/

xxxii

Janet Chang, "How One Year of Microdosing Helped My Career, Relationships, and Happiness," Better Humans, September 21, 2017, https://betterhumans.coach.me/how-one-year-of-microdosing-helped-my-career-relationships-and-happiness-715dbccdfae4 xxxiii

James Fadiman, The Psychedelic Explorer's Guide: Safe, Therapeutic, and Sacred Journeys (Rochester, VT: Park Street Press, 2011)
xxxiv

Rosalind Stone, ""Nobody Knows I'm a Mermaid:" There's More to Microdosing than Productivity," The Third Wave, June 23, 2017, https://thethirdwave.co/microdosing-life-lessons/
xxxv

James Fadiman, The Psychedelic Explorer's Guide: Safe, Therapeutic, and Sacred Journeys (Rochester, VT: Park Street Press, 2011)
xxxvi

UnlimitedMinds, "Preparing truffle capsules for Microdosing," Third Wave forum post, July 17, 2017, https://forum.thethirdwave.co/threads/preparing-truffle-capsules-for-microdosing.121/
xxxvii

http://www.psychedelicexplorersguide.com/
xxxviii

https://www.youtube.com/watch?v=JBgKRyRCVFM
xxxix

https://www.psychologytoday.com/blog/obsessively-yours/201001/five-reasons-not-take-ssris
xl

http://www.medpagetoday.com/Psychiatry/GeneralPsychiatry/17785
xli

http://www.nytimes.com/2010/01/12/health/12ment.html?ref=health
xlii

Shamsah B. Sonawalla, Jerrold F. Rosenbaum, MD, Placebo response in depression, Department of Psychiatry, Massachusetts General Hospital, Harvard Medical School, Boston, Mass, https://www.ncbi.nlm.nih.gov/pmc/articles/PMC3181672/. March 2002
xliii

http://robertwhitaker.org/robertwhitaker.org/Anatomy%20of%20an%20Epidemic.html
xliv

http://www.rollingstone.com/culture/features/how-lsd-microdosing-became-the-hot-new-business-trip-20151120
xlv

http://www.wired.co.uk/article/lsd-microdosing-drugs-silicon-valley
xlvi

http://www.wweek.com/culture/2017/04/18/can-lsd-make-you-better-at-your-job-the-guy-in-the-cubicle-next-to-you-might-be-trying-it/
xlvii

https://thepanelist.net/struggling-with-depression-in-silicon-valley/
xlviii

http://money.cnn.com/mostly-human/silicon-valleys-secret/
xlix

https://www.amazon.com/Really-Good-Day-Microdosing-Difference/dp/0451494091
l

https://thethirdwave.co/ayelet-waldman-really-good-day/
li

https://www.nytimes.com/2017/01/07/style/microdosing-lsd-ayelet-waldman-michael-chabon-marriage.html
lii

https://www.theguardian.com/global/2017/jan/08/how-dropping-acid-saved-my-life-ayelet-waldman-books-depression
liii

http://www.today.com/video/lsd-in-microdoses-can-improve-mood-productivity-some-claim-872494659553
liv

http://www.newyorker.com/culture/persons-of-interest/how-ayelet-waldman-found-a-calmer-life-on-tiny-doses-of-lsd
lv

"Diminished alcohol craving!" Reddit, accessed October 6, 2017, https://www.reddit.com/r/microdosing/comments/71i1c8/diminished_alcohol_craving/
lvi

MAPS, "James Fadiman & Sophia Korb: Microdosing - The Phenomenon, Research Results & Startling Surprises," YouTube, April 26, 2017, https://www.youtube.com/watch?v=JBgKRyRCVFM
lvii

Emma Hogan, "Turn On, Tune In, Drop By the Office," The Economist 1843, August/September, 2017, https://www.1843magazine.com/features/turn-on-tune-in-drop-by-the-office
lviii

"7 Months Microdosing. Full Report, Experiences and Thoughts," Reddit, accessed October 6, 2017,
https://www.reddit.com/r/microdosing/comments/38sef1/7_months_microdosing_full_report_experiences_and/
lix

"Microdosing revisited, effects on athletic performance/intense cardio?" Reddit, accessed October 6, 2017,
https://www.reddit.com/r/microdosing/comments/67bsf4/microdosing_revisited_effects_on_athletic/
lx

"I decided to start sprinting/running on LSD," Reddit, accessed October 6, 2017,
https://www.reddit.com/r/LSD/comments/2i353x/i_decided_to_start_sprintingrunning_on_lsd/
lxi

James Fadiman, The Psychedelic Explorer's Guide: Safe, Therapeutic, and Sacred Journeys (Rochester, VT: Park Street Press, 2011)

Chapter 4: Cautions and Drawbacks

Understandably, experiences like those described in the previous chapters have attracted a great deal of interest in microdosing. But this widespread media attention has also resulted in a glut of reactionary headlines – often unsubstantiated by the articles themselves – linking microdosing to the risk of death and even acid "flashbacks," among other things.

These claims are mostly baseless, but that's actually the point; microdosing is a (relatively) new and understudied trend. It's easy to get caught up in the hype, however well deserved it is, and forget about the potential risks.

Certainly there's a need for more research into the side effects and risks of microdosing. But there are some things we already know. In this chapter, we'll look at the downsides of microdosing and offer cautions and tips for avoiding possible pitfalls.

Keep in mind, however, that I'm not a scientist or a physician and, in any case, the long-term effects of microdosing have never been studied in detail. As Jim Fadiman puts it, what we're doing is gradually filling in a map of an otherwise vast, uncharted territory. To this end, we're forced to rely heavily on anecdotal reports.

Legality

The most obvious drawback to microdosing with psychedelics, and arguably the biggest risk, is that it tends to be illegal – especially when it comes to LSD. *New Scientist* pointed this out in July 2017, citing the growing body of evidence to support these substances' relative safety and therapeutic utility. In a brief editorial piece entitled "Tripping up: The real danger of microdosing with LSD,"[lxii] the magazine laid out its position on psychedelics and, in doing so, echoed the views of the wider scientific community. The article called for a more pragmatic, evidence-based approach to drug policy, one that accepts that people use drugs whether they're legal or not. "The risks deserve further attention," the article concludes, "but a serious criminal record shouldn't be one of them."

Recent developments signal possible change in how western governments handle LSD cases. In September 2017, Norway's Supreme Court overturned an initial five-month prison sentence for LSD possession, commuting the sentence to 45 hours of community service.[lxiii] Citing LSD's potential health benefits, this case may set an example for other western courts to consider.

Nevertheless, most western governments still criminalize psychedelics. Thus, we must see things as they are – for now at least. And as far as the risks of microdosing go, this is one of the few we know for certain.

In Chapter 7 we'll take a deep dive into the legalities of sourcing psychedelics. Aside from the legal aspects, there may be other risks inherent in microdosing.

Heart problems

The general safety of psilocybin and LSD is well established. Indeed, Albert Hofmann's regular use of LSD, well into old age, didn't seem to do any damage; he died at 102. Furthermore, Jim Fadiman and Sophia Korb have seen not one case of lasting harm among the respondents to their ongoing microdosing survey. But these facts are far from enough to verify the long-term safety of microdosing.

One recurrent concern, for instance, is that repeated activation of 5-HT2B receptors in the heart could lead to valvular heart disease (HVD),[lxiv] a condition requiring surgery. This was the case among a small number of patients who were prescribed the now withdrawn drugs fenfluramine/phentermine (fen-phen) and pergolide (Permax) during the 1990s and 2000s. In fact, fen-phen roughly doubled patients' risk of developing HVD after a 90-day course of treatment at 30 mg/day. Of course,

30 mg is 3,000 times as much as the typical microdose of LSD (10 μg). But the way in which LSD binds to 5-HT2B receptors keeps it "trapped" inside for many hours, possibly accumulating over time.

Some have reported abnormal heart effects in the shorter term as well. One user who took a relatively moderate microdose of 10-15 μg found his heart rate increased immediately, leading to palpitations, pain, and high blood pressure that persisted for months. However, he also had existing anxiety issues, so it's unknown whether these symptoms were due to LSD.

Another study looked at the effects of daily microdoses of psilocin (the main psychoactive form of psilocybin) on rats over a period of three months. Although they claimed to find "cardiac abnormalities," their methodology was flawed and their results lacked any statistical context.

Ultimately, we just don't know much about the long-term cardiac effects of microdosing. For this reason, it's best to limit your microdosing cycles to no more than 90 days at a time, with at least two rest days between each dose and perhaps a month or so between each cycle.

People with existing heart conditions should be especially cautious and perhaps even avoid microdosing altogether – at least until we know more. If this includes you, avoid combining microdoses with caffeine, since this has been known to cause palpitations.

Other specific contraindications

Although microdosing shows great potential for the treatment of bipolar depression, individual symptoms and responses will of course vary. Ayelet Waldman and others may have been able to stabilize their mood swings with LSD, but the potential for over-stimulation suggests it may be less suitable during the mania phase.

Potential interactions with lithium carbonate, a drug commonly prescribed for bipolar disorder, are especially worrying. In his talk at Psychedelic Science 2017,[lxv] Fadiman made specific reference to this medication, stating that he and Korb were unsure about its safety with microdoses of LSD or psilocybin. In fact, combining it with LSD (at macrodoses, at least) can cause seizures and even coma in users with no history of these symptoms – perhaps because both LSD and lithium lower the seizure threshold.

For the same reason, it's probably best to avoid microdosing if you already suffer from seizures. You should also be cautious about combining microdoses with other drugs that appear to lower the seizure threshold. These include certain antiasthmatics, antibiotics, anesthetics, antidepressants, immunosuppressants, and stimulants.[lxvi]

SSRI antidepressants should be avoided not just because they lower the seizure threshold, but also because they reduce the effects of psychedelics. Common SSRIs include fluoxetine (Prozac), paroxetine (Paxil), sertraline (Zoloft), citalopram (Celexa), and trazodone (Desyrel).

Conversely, MAOIs can significantly increase the effects of psychedelics by inhibiting their dissolution in the body. After all, this is why MAOIs are included in the ayahuasca brew. Common MAOIs include the drugs phenelzine (Nardil), isocarboxazid (Marplan), selegiline or L-deprenyl (Eldepryl), moclobemide (Aurorix or Manerix), and furazolidone (Furoxone).

Except insofar as MAOIs' necessary use in ayahuasca, both MAOIs and SSRIs should be avoided to maintain control over your microdoses. And SSRIs should absolutely not be taken in conjunction with ayahuasca, since combining SSRIs and MAOIs can lead to potentially fatal serotonin syndrome.

Iboga is another particularly dangerous psychedelic to combine with other drugs. It's generally recommended that you completely wean off all medications before taking it – especially SSRIs/SNRIs. MAOIs, although relatively little is known about their interaction with ibogaine, should not be taken for at least seven to 10 days beforehand. Once again, if you plan to go off your medications, please consult first with a physician.

If you're planning to microdose alongside prescribed medications, it's important to do your research first. Certainly check with a medical professional, but also seek advice from others who may be in a similar situation. Our online microdosing course and community are excellent resources to start with.

One final, and rather more curious, contraindication should be mentioned here: It appears that people with colorblindness often experience visual distortions, including tracers, after taking LSD microdoses. In Korb and Fadiman's research, five participants dropped out because of these effects. It's not clear why colorblind people in particular are affected, but, if you're one of them, you may want to think twice about microdosing in potentially hazardous situations.

Physical discomfort

Muscle cramps are frequently reported, especially in the neck area, after taking LSD microdoses – possibly due to vasoconstriction. Taking a warm shower or stretching is said to help. It could also be related to a magnesium deficiency, so magnesium supplements could also be useful. In any case, if the discomfort persists you should try lowering your dose.

Gastric issues are also somewhat common, primarily with psilocybin mushrooms but also with LSD and other psychedelics. One user who took LSD microdoses on three consecutive days, for example, woke on the second, third, and fourth days with stomach pains or cramps (although this may be due to a change of diet, catalyzed by the microdosing mindset). Aside from lowering doses and, in this case, spacing them further apart, ginger tea may help to settle the stomach. With psilocybin mushrooms and other plant material, grinding them up for use in capsules can also avoid gastric upset. I'll cover this in detail in Chapter 8.

Anxiety and agitation

As with macrodoses of psychedelics, your mindset going into a microdose could heavily determine the effects. You should therefore be cautious about using them during times of stress and upheaval – not least because microdosing can spotlight your own thoughts, however positive or negative they may be. While a great many people find relief from anxiety or depression through microdosing, this amplification of emotional states may be why others find their symptoms aggravated. If you do choose to microdose during a difficult time, it may be useful to meditate, even for just five or 10 minutes beforehand.

There can be a fine line between high productivity and an inability to focus on any one task. For instance, one user, who experienced a stable increase in energy levels and lower anxiety and depression while microdosing psilocybin mushrooms, had trouble adjusting to LSD. First at 16 µg and then at 10 µg, he found his energy levels were too high after the first hour. He described his mental state as "scatty" and found it a challenge to concentrate on his work and interact with other people. He was also yawning and tired, despite the energy boost. This loss of control, especially at work, could exacerbate anxiety. An obvious solution would be to lower the dose or, if that fails, to stop microdosing altogether.

Some people have trouble sleeping at night, even if they microdose in the morning. This is especially common with LSD due to its longer duration. If you find this to be a problem, it may be worth switching to psilocybin. On the other hand, microdosing can also lead to fatigue or extreme tiredness when the immediate effects have faded. While some report an afterglow effect that persists for a day or two, others report exhaustion, irritability, and even depression in the days that follow, especially when microdosing more than twice a week. Agitation and irritability also appear to be a problem with iboga, perhaps because it can accumulate over time in the body.

Some of these effects might point to the need for a change in lifestyle, which is after all what microdosing is supposed to assist with. So pay close attention to your diet, sleeping pattern, exercise regimen, and other things that could be affecting your mood and energy levels.

Manic states

As author and flow-state authority Steven Kotler said in his interview with The Third Wave Podcast, "the difference between flow and mania is a thin line." In other words, the impulsivity that microdosing gives rise to can be fantastic in many ways – indeed it's one of microdosing's appeals – but it can also lead to poor judgment and making decisions you may later regret. For example you might say something you probably shouldn't have, agree to a business project you'd rather have thought more about, or buy unnecessary things that you wouldn't usually buy (something I know all too well from personal experience).

We look at some ways to mitigate this risk in Chapter 10, but underlying them all is the necessity for conscious self-awareness whenever you take a microdose.

Dodgy suppliers

Often, you won't know the precise dose that you're taking – especially in the case of LSD, since doses can be considerably more or less potent than advertised. As a result, you may experience inconsistent effects and even full-blown trips, which are obviously problematic if you're at work or driving. That's why it's always important to start out with small doses (5-6 μg), and to be cautious with each new supply. You should also avoid microdosing at work, and especially in potentially hazardous situations, until you're aware of and comfortable with the effects of your dose.

That said, sometimes not knowing the precise dose you're taking is the least of your worries when it comes to sampling new substances. Assuming you don't get caught or arrested in the process of sourcing them, the lack of regulation means you can't even be sure what you're getting. Again, this is especially true in the case of LSD, which is sometimes substituted with the potentially very dangerous 25I-NBO-Me. Many powdered extracts and whole plants, if you're not familiar with them, can easily be mis-sold as well. There's also the risk of misidentifying substances in the wild – particularly mushrooms, which can be deadly if you get the wrong type.

Mixing microdosing with drugs and supplements

Participants in the microdosing study (using LSD, 1p-LSD, or psilocybin) have reported using these medications and supplements with no adverse response.

Painkillers
- Acetaminophen/paracetemol (Tylenol)
- Aspirin
- Codeine
- Dihydrocodeine (Co-dydramol)
- Hydrocodone (Vicodin, Norco)
- Ibuprofen (Advil, Motrin)
- Naproxen (Aleve)
- Tramadol (Ultram)

Heart/high blood pressure medication
- Amiodarone (Cordarone, Nexterone)
- Hydrochlorothiazide (HCTZ, HCT)
- Lisinopril (Prinivil, Zestril)
- Losartan (Cozaar)
- Spironolactone (Aldactone)
- Telmisartan (Micardis, Actavis)
- Valsartan (Diovan)

Birth control
- Aubra
- Hormonal pills
- Marvelon
- Mirena
- Nuva ring
- Tricyclen
- Antacid
- Ranitidine (Zantac)

Antibiotics
- Clindamycin (Cleocin, Dalacin, Clinacin)
- Doxycycline
- Minocycline (Minocin, Minomycin, Akamin)
- Penicillin (Bicillin)
- Antifungals
- Fluconazole (Diflucan, Celozole)

Focus meds (ADHD/ADD)
- Amphetamine (Adderall)
- Bupropion (Wellbutrin)
- Dextroamphetamine (Dexedrine, Metamina, Attentin, Zenzedi, Procentra, Amfexa)
- Lisdexamfetamine (Vyvanse)
- Methylphenidate (Ritalin, Biphentin)
- Modafinil (Provigil)

Sleeping
- Zopiclone (Zimovane, Imovane)
- Melatonin
- Zolpidem (ambien, stilnox)

Antihistamines
- Cetirizine (Zyrtec)
- Diphenahydramine (Benadryl, Gravol)

- Loratadine (Claritin)
- Ranitidine (Zantac)

Benzodiazepines (Anxiety, sleep, seizure)
- Alprazolam (Xanax)
- Clonazepam (Klonopin)
- Diazepam (Valium)
- Flurazepam (Staurodorm)
- Lorazepam (Ativan)

Other anxiolytics
- Etizolam
- Propranolol
- Parkinsons
- Levodopa
- Pramipexole

Cholesterol
- Atorvastatin (Lipitor)
- Rosuvastatin (Crestor)
- Simvastatin (Zocor)
- Statins
- Racetams
- Aniracetam
- Phenylpiracetam
- Piracetam

Mood stabilizers and antipsychotics
- Aripiprazole (Abilify)
- Buspirone (Buspar)
- lamotrigine (Lamictal)
- Lithium
- Quetiapine (Seroquel)
- Diabetes
- Metformin (Glucophage)
- Anticonvulsants

- Baclofen (Lioresal)
- Carbamazepine (Tegretol)
- Cyclobenzaprine (Flexeril)
- Gabapentin
- Mirtazapine
- Sodium valproate
- Tizanidine (Zanaflex)

Thyroid

- Methimazole or Thiamazole

Antidepressants

- Bupropion (Wellbutrin)
- Citalopram (Celexa)
- Desvenlafaxine (Pristiq)
- Doxepin (Sinequan)
- Duloxetine (Cymbalta)
- Escitalopram (Lexapro)
- Paroxetine (Paxil)
- Sertraline (Zoloft)
- Venlafaxine (Effexor)

GERD

- Esomeprazole (Nexium)
- Pantoprazole (Protonix)
- Ranitidine (Zantac)

Breathing (asthma, COPD)

- Salbutamol (Albuterol)
- Cetirizine (Zyrtec)
- Beclometasone (Clenil Modulite)
- Montelukast (Singulair)
- Antiviral
- Nitazoxanide

Drugs of recreation

- Alcohol
- Amphetamine
- Heroin
- Kratom
- Marijuana
- Nicotine

Anti-inflammatory

- Mesalazine (Octasa)

Immunosuppressant

- Hydroxychloroquine (Quensyl)
- Erectile Dysfunction
- Tadalafil (Cialis)

Alcohol dependence treatment

- Acamprosate (Campral)
- Disulfiram (Antabuse)
- Naltrexone

Hormones and Steroids

- Norethindrone Acetate ethinyl estradiol
- Estradiol
- Prednisone (Deltasone, Liquid Pred, Orasone, Adasone, Deltacortisone)
- Estrogen (Premarin)
- Progesterone (Prometrium, Utrogestan, Endometrin)
- Testosterone
- Levothyroxine (Synthroid)
- Naturethroid
- Dexamethasone
- DHEA
- Spironolactone (Aldactone)

Supplements

- 5-HTP

- Albizia
- Ashwagha
- B100
- BCAAs
- Biotin
- Brahmi
- Bromelain
- Caffeine
- Calcium
- Cannabis
- Dayenne
- Chaga
- Chlorophyll
- Choline
- CILTEP
- CoQ10
- Cordycepts
- Creatine
- Eleuthero
- EPA/DHA
- Fish oil
- Ginseng
- Glucosamine
- Iodine
- Iron
- Kelp
- Kratom
- L-theanine
- Lemon balm
- Lions mane
- Maca
- Magnesium
- MCT
- Methyl sulfonyl methane (MSM)
- Milk thistle
- Multivitamins

- Omega 3/6/9
- Passionflower
- Phosphatidyl
- Probiotics
- Pycnogenol
- Reishi
- Rhodiola
- Rosacea
- Selenium
- Shatavari
- Skullcap
- St. Johns wort
- Taurine
- Tulsi
- Turmeric (curcumin)
- Turkey tail
- Twynsta

Vitamins
- B6
- B12
- D3
- K
- C
- K2
- D
- Zinc
- Zinium

Weighing the risks

Microdosing isn't for everybody. Your experiences with a substance will always be different from the experiences of others.

To mitigate the downsides as far as possible, keep in mind the following tips for the standard protocol:

- Don't microdose at work until you have calibrated your dosage appropriately
- Start low and go slow, gradually increasing the dose from the minimum
- Restrict your use to twice per week to avoid tolerance build-up and attachment to the effects
- Limit your protocol to 90 days and then take a break
- Always test your drugs!

As we continue to find out how and why microdosing affects people, you can become an early test subject by participating. Only you can decide whether the benefits outweigh the risks – but do so with the understanding that we do not have absolute clarity on the long-term effects.

---

lxii

"Tripping up: The real danger of microdosing with LSD," *New Scientist,* June 14, 2017, https://www.newscientist.com/article/mg23431303-300-tripping-up-the-real-danger-of-microdosing-with-lsd/
lxiii

"LSD's Health Benefits Convince Norway to Relax Punishment For Possession While America continues to resist," Tonic, Oct 6 2017, https://tonic.vice.com/en_us/article/ne7m4m/lsds-health-benefits-norway-possession
lxiv

"Microdosing with LSD and its Research Potential," *Heffter Research Institute*, August 17, 2017, http://heffter.org/microdosing-lsd-research-potential/
lxv

MAPS, "James Fadiman & Sophia Korb: Microdosing - The Phenomenon, Research Results & Startling Surprises," *YouTube*, April 26, 2017, https://www.youtube.com/watch?v=JBgKRyRCVFM
lxvi

E. B. Bromfield,"Drugs that May Lower Seizure Threshold," *Epilepsy Foundation*, accessed on October 8, 2017, http://www.epilepsy.com/learn/professionals/resource-library/tables/drugs-may-lower-seizure-threshold

Chapter 5: The Science of Microdosing (so far)

The science is still catching up on exactly how microdosing affects the brain, but by taking a critical look at the research that is out there we can form a cohesive hypothesis on what is occurring. When I invited neuroscientist Zach Mainen, Ph.D., onto The Third Wave Podcast, we talked about how serotonin is likely the key to understanding psychedelics – and moreover how microdosing could be effecting such powerful transformations in people's lives.

Serotonin is one of the most important neurotransmitters we have, distributed throughout the body and involved in many diverse functions – including mood, sleep, memory, and cognition. Many antidepressants work by inhibiting the reuptake (reabsorption) of serotonin in the brain, thereby increasing its availability.

The effects of LSD, psilocybin, and other typical psychedelics also involve this neurotransmitter, but through a very different mechanism of action. Like serotonin itself, they bind to or stimulate serotonin receptors – primarily the subtype known as 5-HT2A. This leads to (among other things) increases in:

- production of BDNF (brain-derived neurotrophic factor), a protein that nurtures existing neurons and promotes the genesis of new ones; and
- transmission of glutamate, a neurotransmitter involved in cognition, learning, and memory[lxvii].

Although we're still learning about these effects and their interaction with one another, they have clear implications for microdosing. Many of us experience greater neuroplasticity, more rapid learning, and better overall cognitive functioning as a result of our experiments.

In talking about serotonin receptors more generally, Mainen described two of his own studies on mice.

In the first, he paired a specific odor with a reward, such as water, to condition the mice to expect that reward whenever they smelled the odor. Later, his team either removed the reward or replaced it with a punishment: a puff of air to the face. The mice were therefore compelled to re-associate the odor with a new outcome – a difficult task for any animal since it requires not only overwriting the original association (relearning/plasticity) but also withholding their normal response (impulse control). Interestingly, this task was made even more difficult when serotonin receptors were blocked.

In the second of Mainen's experiments on mice, he observed their behavior in a controlled environment – first under normal circumstances and then when serotonin was stimulated in brief, repeated pulses lasting no more than a few seconds each. In the latter case the movement of the mice was slowed by around half, and they showed less signs of jumpiness or impulsivity, an effect supported by numerous other studies.

Both of these experiments suggest a strong link between serotonin and patience or impulse control, adaptability, and neuroplasticity – all of which are observed among microdosers.

Creating new connections in the brain

We could hypothesize on the basis of what we know that consistent activation of serotonin receptors (including 5-HT2A) through regular microdosing could effectively alter the functioning of the brain. It could potentially deconstruct negative thought patterns and establish new, more beneficial neural pathways. This might explain the patience, receptivity, presence, mindfulness, and adaptability to new ideas that we've seen or experienced from microdosing.

Psychedelics are also thought to disrupt the default mode network (DMN), the part of the brain that is active when people aren't engaged in any particular project or activity. The DMN essentially takes you out of the present moment and triggers daydreams, memory recall, planning for the future, wondering about the intentions of other people, and other states that can be useful in some circumstances but can also trap people in persistent patterns of anxiety or depression.[lxviii]

By bypassing old connections in the brain and creating new ones, psychedelics allow people to step away from harmful patterns and non-productive thoughts, and build up a more fruitful state of being.[lxix]

Disrupting the DMN also helps people be more grounded in the present moment, achieving a state of mindfulness useful for battling depression.[lxx] Mindfulness allows people to observe their thoughts and emotions without becoming attached to them, meaning they are less affected by negativity or preoccupations. The state of mindfulness is most commonly associated with meditation, but taking psychedelics can help achieve a similar result, and many people combine both to find peace in their body and mind.[lxxi]

The growing number of studies that show how and why full doses of LSD and psilocybin work to mitigate depression, anxiety, and other mental disorders can help further our understanding of why they could have a similar effect for microdosers. Author Michael Pollan, famous for his books on the history, culture, and ethics of food production, contributed a huge advancement to the mainstreaming of psychedelics with a 2015 *New Yorker* article about research being conducted to combat mental disorders.[lxxii]

The first clinical study on LSD as a therapy in four decades was published in 2014, encompassing four years of data collected between 2008 and 2012 on how the chemical affected anxiety.[lxxiii] Twelve participants who were near the end of their lives were provided LSD-assisted psychotherapy and subsequently interviewed about their responses. The result, the study concluded, was that anxiety "went down and stayed down."

"My LSD experience brought back some lost emotions and ability to trust, lots of psychological insights, and a timeless moment when the universe didn't seem like a trap, but like a revelation of utter beauty," one of the participants said.

Beyond anxiety and depression, other research has shown that psychedelics can also be effective in treating substance abuse, perhaps for similar reasons. A 2012 review and meta-analysis of several studies, some conducted in the 1970s or earlier, found that "a single dose of LSD, in the context of various alcoholism treatment programs, is associated with a decrease in alcohol misuse."[lxxiv] Certainly anecdotal reports by people who have used psychedelics to combat addiction suggest that feelings of connectivity, gratitude, and beauty have helped them move past their addiction. In other words, people who are able to address the root causes of problems such as anxiety and depression should have an easier time avoiding getting trapped in cycles of addiction.

Scientists at Imperial College London (ICL) recently produced a study in which they scanned the brains of subjects who had taken LSD, finding a huge boost in connectivity.[lxxv] Researcher Robin Carhart-Harris explained the results: "Normally our brain consists of independent networks that perform separate specialised functions, such as vision, movement and hearing – as well as more complex things like attention. However, under LSD the separateness of these networks breaks down and instead you see a more integrated or unified brain."

"Our results suggest that this effect underlies the profound altered state of consciousness that people often describe during an LSD experience," Carhart-Harris continued. "It is also related to what people sometimes call 'ego-dissolution,' which means the normal sense of self is broken down and replaced by a sense of reconnection with themselves, others and the natural world. This experience is sometimes framed in a religious or spiritual way – and seems to be associated with improvements in well-being after the drug's effects have subsided."[lxxvi]

Psilocybin studies

One study that helped kick off the current wave of psychedelic research, published in 2006, found that psilocybin was helpful to people trying to overcome obsessive-compulsive disorder.[lxxvii] The research was initially intended to focus on the safety of psilocybin, leaving it up to future scientists to discover its effectiveness, but the positive effects were impossible to ignore. "Marked decreases in OCD symptoms of variable degrees were observed in all subjects during 1 or more of the testing sessions," the study reported. "Improvement generally lasted past the 24-hour timepoint."

Another trial conducted on mice found that animals trained to fear certain stimuli were able to overcome the fear conditioning more quickly when given low doses of psilocybin.[lxxviii]

More recently, a study published in 2016 found evidence that psilocybin could be effective against treatment-resistant depression.[lxxix] Out of 12 subjects who suffered from severe or very severe depression, all showed a reduction in symptoms for at least a week after being administered psilocybin, with a majority still feeling positive effects three months later. "The magnitude and duration of the post-treatment reductions in symptom severity motivate further controlled research," the study concludes. "Psilocybin has a novel pharmacological action in comparison with currently available treatments for depression and thus could constitute a useful addition to available therapies for the treatment of depression."

Quite a few studies have focused on using psilocybin to reduce anxiety and other problems such as depression and psychological distress in cancer patients. Research carried out at the Harbor-UCLA Medical Center, Johns Hopkins, and New York University all found that the substance could have profound and even transformative effects on people facing the end of their lives.

A pilot study at UCLA established that it was safe to administer psilocybin to cancer patients, and provided a roadmap forward with results that suggested mood improvement.[lxxx] At Hopkins, 80 percent of participants felt reductions in anxiety and depression after undergoing psilocybin-assisted therapy, and 67 percent went so far as to call it one of the top five meaningful experiences in their lives.[lxxxi] "The most interesting and remarkable finding is that a single dose of psilocybin, which lasts four to six hours, produced enduring decreases in depression and anxiety symptoms, and this may represent a fascinating new model for treating some psychiatric conditions," said researcher Roland Griffiths.

NYU reported similar results, concluding the treatment "produced rapid and sustained anxiolytic and antidepressant effects (for at least 7 weeks but potentially as long as 8 months), decreased cancer-related existential distress, increased spiritual wellbeing and quality of life, and was associated with improved attitudes towards death . . . Psilocybin, administered in conjunction with appropriate psychotherapy, could become a novel pharmacological-psychosocial treatment modality for cancer-related psychological and existential distress."[lxxxii]

One of the study subjects at UCLA, neuropsychologist Annie Levy, spoke of her battle with ovarian cancer and how psilocybin helped her come to terms with her fear. "As soon as it started working I knew I had nothing to be afraid of because it connected me with the universe," she said of her experience, saying she was then able to better see and appreciate her relationships with her loved ones.

"I would recommend psilocybin treatment for anyone with a terminal or potentially terminal illness," she said. "It's more helpful than any other treatment I've ever had."[lxxxiii]

Lauri Kershman, MD, was a leukemia patient who took psilocybin as part of the Johns Hopkins study. "The impact that the study had on my life was enormous," she said. "The safety that I felt to be able to let go and face some demons and go deep into some pretty difficult and sad places."[lxxxiv]

Just as it has for LSD, ICL has led the way in using brain scans to help understand how psilocybin affects the brain. One study revealed how psilocybin facilitates neural connections that are otherwise not present or neglected.[lxxxv] "A simple reading of this result would be that the effect of psilocybin is to relax the constraints on brain function, ascribing cognition a more flexible quality, but when looking at the edge level, the picture becomes more complex," the study's discussion section states. "The brain does not simply become a random system after psilocybin injection, but instead retains some organizational features, albeit different from the normal state, as suggested by the first part of the analysis. Further work is required to identify the exact functional significance of these edges."

Another brain mapping study at ICL found that psilocybin helped stimulate activity in the hippocampus and anterior cingulate cortex, parts of the brain linked to emotional thinking that are often active during dreams.[lxxxvi] "What we have done in this research is begin to identify the biological basis of the reported mind expansion associated with psychedelic drugs," researcher Carhart-Harris said of the study. "I was fascinated to see similarities between the pattern of brain activity in a psychedelic state and the pattern of brain activity during dream sleep, especially as both involve the primitive areas of the brain linked to emotions and memory. People often describe taking psilocybin as producing a dream-like state and our findings have, for the first time, provided a physical representation for the experience in the brain."

Microdosing and psychotherapy

As we close this chapter, it's important to keep in mind that most of the studies I just described combine full doses of psychedelics with therapy for maximum results. Yet, anecdotally we know that for some people microdosing has worked the same way. "My microdosing has been in conjunction with therapy to address my depression/anxiety issues so my positive results have been a two-pronged attack on these issues," a Third Wave reader wrote in. "I have had therapy by itself in the past and the results I have found this time have been much more groundbreaking for me and in a much more timely manner. There are a lot of variables with these results but I truly believe that microdosing has been an integral part of the positive outcome for these issues."

The sheer extent of evidence showing that LSD and psilocybin can be helpful for mental disorders helps explain why many people find microdosing with the substances to be productive.

The existing research on psychedelics is compelling, all the more so given the difficulty of conducting studies with Schedule I substances that are strictly controlled under federal law. Microdosing is even harder to examine today, because any practical study would require the subjects to actually possess the substances and administer them to themselves – something that federal authorities would likely never allow. A potential loosening of legal restrictions could mean a vast wave of new research that provides us with even more understanding about what these chemicals can do and how they act on the human brain – which could include revealing research on how microdosing can offer positive mental health effects, and even, as some people have reported, save lives.

---

lxvii

Ayelet Waldman, *A Really Good Day: How Microdosing Made a Mega Difference in My Mood, My Marriage, and My Life* (New York: Knopf Publishing Group, 2017)
lxviii

"Know your brain: Default mode network," *Neuroscientifically Challenged*, June 16, 2015, http://www.neuroscientificallychallenged.com/blog/know-your-brain-default-mode-network
lxix

Andrea Anderson, "LSD May Chip Away at the Brain's "Sense of Self" Network," *Scientific American*, April 13, 2016, https://www.scientificamerican.com/article/lsd-may-chip-away-at-the-brain-s-sense-of-self-network/
lxx

Milan Scheidegger, Psilocybin Enhances Mindfulness-Related Capabilities in a Meditation Retreat Setting: A Double-Blind Placebo-Controlled fMRI Study, Filmed at Psychedelic Science 2017, Video,http://psychedelicscience.org/conference/interdisciplinary/psilocybin-enhances-mindfulness-related-capabilities-in-a-meditation-retreat-setting-a-double-blind-placebo-controlled-fmri-study
lxxi

Vanja Palmers, "Meditation and Psychedelics," *MAPS* volume XI, number 2 (fall 2001): 43-44,
http://www.maps.org/news-letters/v11n2/11243pal.html
lxxii

Michael Pollan, "The Trip Treatment," *The New Yorker*, February 9, 2015,
http://www.newyorker.com/magazine/2015/02/09/trip-treatment
lxxiii

Peter Gasser, Dominique Holstein, Yvonne Michel, Rick Doblin, Berra Yazar-Klosinski, Torsten
Passie, and Rudolf Brenneisen, "Safety and Efficacy of Lysergic Acid Diethylamide-Assisted
Psychotherapy for Anxiety Associated With Life-threatening Diseases," *The Journal of Nervous
and Mental Disease* 202, no. 7 (July 2014): 513-20.
http://journals.lww.com/jonmd/Documents/90000000.0-00001.pdf
lxxiv

Teri S Krebs, Pål-Ørjan Johansen, "Lysergic acid diethylamide (LSD) for alcoholism: meta-analysis
of randomized controlled trials," *Journal of Psychopharmacology* 26, no. 7 (March 2012): 994-
1002.http://journals.sagepub.com/doi/abs/10.1177/0269881112439253
lxxv

Robin L. Carhart-Harris, Suresh Muthukumaraswamy, Leor Roseman, Mendel Kaelen, Wouter
Droog, Kevin Murphy, Enzo Tagliazucchi et al., "Neural correlates of the LSD experience revealed
by multimodal neuroimaging," *PNAS* 113, no. 17 (April 2016): 4853-58.
http://www.pnas.org/content/113/17/4853.full.pdf
lxxvi

Kate Wighton, "The brain on LSD revealed: first scans show how the drug affects the brain,"
Imperial College London *News*, April 11, 2016,
http://www3.imperial.ac.uk/newsandeventspggrp/imperialcollege/newssummary/news_11-4-2016-
17-21-2
lxxvii

Moreno FA, Wiegand CB, Taitano EK, Delgado PL, "Safety, tolerability, and efficacy of
psilocybin in 9 patients with obsessive-compulsive disorder," *Journal of Clinical Psychiatry* 67, no.
11 (November 2006): 1735-40. https://www.ncbi.nlm.nih.gov/pubmed/17196053
lxxviii

Briony J. Catlow, Shijie Song, Daniel A. Paredes, Cheryl L. Kirstein, Juan Sanchez-Ramos,
"Effects of psilocybin on hippocampal neurogenesis and extinction of trace fear conditioning,"
Experimental Brain Research 228, no. 4 (August 2013): 481-91.
https://www.ncbi.nlm.nih.gov/pubmed/23727882

lxxix

Robin L Carhart-Harris, Mark Bolstridge, James Rucker, Camilla M J Day, David Erritzoe, Mendel Kaelen, Michael Bloomfield et al., "Psilocybin with psychological support for treatment-resistant depression: an open-label feasibility study," *Lancet Psychiatry* 3 (May 2016): 619-27. http://www.thelancet.com/pdfs/journals/lanpsy/PIIS2215-0366(16)30065-7.pdf

lxxx

Charles S. Grob, Alicia L. Danforth, Gurpreet S. Chopra, "Pilot Study of Psilocybin Treatment for Anxiety in Patients With Advanced-Stage Cancer," *Archives of General Psychiatry* 68, no. 1 (January 2011): 71-78 http://jamanetwork.com/journals/jamapsychiatry/fullarticle/210962

lxxxi

Vanessa McMains, "Hallucinogenic drug found in 'magic mushrooms' eases depression, anxiety in people with life-threatening cancer," *Johns Hopkins Magazine*, December 1, 2016, https://hub.jhu.edu/2016/12/01/hallucinogen-treats-cancer-depression-anxiety/

lxxxii

Stephen Ross, Anthony Bossis, Jeffrey Guss, Gabrielle Agin-Liebes, Tara Malone, Barry Cohen, Sarah E Menneng et al., "Rapid and sustained symptom reduction following psilocybin treatment for anxiety and depression in patients with life-threatening cancer: a randomized controlled trial," *Journal of Psychopharmacology* 30, no. 12 (2016): 1165-80. http://journals.sagepub.com/doi/pdf/10.1177/0269881116675512

lxxxiii

Heffter Research Institute, "Annie Levy - Psilocybin Study Participant," video, October 26, 2014, https://www.youtube.com/watch?v=xYhtXI4Prpo&feature=youtu.be

lxxxiv

Heffter Research Institute, "Kershman: Benefits from the Johns Hopkins Psilocybin Study," video, March 14, 2014, https://www.youtube.com/watch?v=OefUwXIKj90&feature=youtu.be

lxxxv

G. Petri, P. Expert, F. Turkheimer, R. Carhart-Harris, D. Nutt, P. J. Hellyer, F. Vaccarino, "Homological scaffolds of brain functional networks," *Journal of the Royal Society Interface* 11, no. 101 (October 2014). http://rsif.royalsocietypublishing.org/content/11/101/20140873

lxxxvi

Francesca Davenport, New study discovers biological basis for magic mushroom 'mind expansion'," Imperial College London *News*, July 3, 2014,

73

http://www3.imperial.ac.uk/newsandeventspggrp/imperialcollege/newssummary/news_2-7-2014-18-11-12

Chapter 6: Microdosing in Technology and Entrepreneurial Circles

Now that we've covered the science of microdosing – how it works – as well as its benefits, history, and potential drawbacks, let's take a look at *why* so many leaders in business and tech find the practice appealing. In this case, I'll begin with the business leader I know best: Me.

As an entrepreneur in search of a better way to approach work, avoid procrastination, and boost my productivity, I began microdosing in July 2015, around the time the media was picking up on the practice and other entrepreneurs were tuning in as well. Prior to that, knowledge of microdosing was limited to very small circles. This widespread growth in recognition did not come out of nowhere. Rather, the spread of microdosing in large part stems from its popularity among some of the most powerful and innovative tech entrepreneurs in Silicon Valley.

Author and venture capitalist Tim Ferriss provided an insightful look inside Silicon Valley culture that suggests profound implications for the future of microdosing. "The billionaires I know, almost without exception, use hallucinogens on a regular basis," Ferriss told CNN *Money*. "[They're] trying to be very disruptive and look at the problems in the world ... and ask completely new questions."[lxxxvii]

Indeed, Apple co-founder Steve Jobs famously claimed that taking LSD was such a profound experience that it ranked as one of the most important things he ever did in his life. Considering his success in business, that's a powerful statement. But if it's tempting to dismiss Jobs as an outlier, a visionary fated for great accomplishments no matter what his formative experiences, it's more difficult to ignore the sheer volume of reports on how completely psychedelics in general, and now microdosing specifically, have permeated the culture and workforce in Silicon Valley and therefore play a role in the development of many of the apps and products that people around the world use every day.

Because psychedelics are still illegal under federal and state laws in the U.S., many people are reluctant to speak publicly about their use, but word is getting out nevertheless. As I recounted in earlier chapters, stories in *Rolling Stone, Wired, Forbes,* BBC, the *New York Times,* the *Washington Post,* the *Guardian,* and *GQ* have all described a growing trend that is all but out in the open.

Some people are willing to go on the record. Longtime Cisco engineer Kevin Herbert acknowledged to CNN that using LSD helped him solve complicated work problems, and many of his younger colleagues also use psychedelics to improve their output and creativity.[lxxxviii] The practice is also gaining an ever-growing chorus of true believers in other high-profile fields as well, lauded by athletes, actors, and writers for helping to break out of ruts and achieve new levels of performance.

The prevalence of psychedelic use among some of the most prominent and successful people in Silicon Valley has potential to make a dramatic impact on the substances' standing worldwide. As more and more people acknowledge that they have tried microdosing and found it useful – and sometimes even transformative – psychedelics may be able to shed the stigma they acquired through decades of negative propaganda proffered by the media and the U.S. government.

The more people speak about microdosing and using psychedelics in general, the further the concept wedges itself into mainstream thought, not as something subversive or dangerous, but as a useful tool to help unlock human effectiveness.

In fact, the declarations of profound benefits by executives and celebrities are consistent with anecdotal reports provided to The Third Wave by individuals who have tried microdosing to help with their own personal or professional goals. One reader described intense focus during writing sessions while microdosing:

"I am very focused for 2-4 hours, depending on how tired I am leading up to the dose. During the dose, I'm very, very slightly loopy – my thoughts are mostly coherent and streamlined, but I usually wait until I'm sober again to double-check my work. One noticeable difference is that, when I write to the point that I need to fact-check or research something, I will do that and then return to writing. Ordinarily, this can either halt my flow, or I will add a marker and come back to it."

Another contributor noted, "I can focus more easily on complex tasks such as writing an essay as I can almost 'feel' how my thoughts move through my hand on to my pen and then on to the paper."

The Long Partnership of Psychedelics and Tech

Silicon Valley is a natural location for the epicenter of microdosing, given that the Bay Area was a hotbed of legal LSD experimentation prior to federal prohibition. Like Steve Jobs, many of the same people who became giants in the tech field used LSD in their formative years prior to developing breakthrough computer technologies. Microdosing and the connection between psychedelics and high tech is in effect a continuation of a relationship that has been ongoing for more than 60 years. "From the start, a small but significant crossover existed between those who were experimenting with drugs and the burgeoning tech community in San Francisco," reports the *Economist's 1843 Magazine.*[lxxxix]

In the book *What the Dormouse Said*, journalist John Markoff relates the close history between psychedelics and software engineers and how the Bay Area counterculture of the '60s and '70s, steeped with LSD, bled over into the nascent tech scene.[xc] In one example, Doug Engelbart, a veteran of the International Foundation for Advanced Study's LSD experiments, went on to found the Augmented Human Intellect Research Center at the Stanford Research Institute. Among his game-changing innovations was the computer mouse. What's more, the idealism found in pioneers who envisioned computers as a tool to empower the individual with egalitarian access to information is rather reminiscent of aspirations frequently attached to psychedelic consumption – to free human minds from their constraints. Arguably, LSD played an important role in the development of the personal computer, which went on to irrevocably alter the very nature of work and human interactions in the ensuing decades.[xci]

The popularity of psychedelics in Silicon Valley is also evidenced in gatherings like Burning Man. During the extended art fest held annually in the Nevada desert, many in attendance express their creativity and culture in a non-judgmental environment, with psychedelics as an essential ingredient. "If you haven't been, you just don't get Silicon Valley," groundbreaking entrepreneur Elon Musk said in an interview with Re/Code. "You could take the craziest L.A. party and multiply it by a thousand, and it doesn't even get fucking close."[xcii]

Google CEO Larry Page corroborated the connection between dreaming up better ways of solving computer problems and performing art in the desert. "I like going to Burning Man," Page said at the Google I/O conference. "An environment where people can change new things. I think as technologists we should have some safe places where we can try out new things and figure out the effect on society. What's the effect on people, without having to deploy it to the whole world."[xciii]

As discussed earlier, in addition to its claim as the center of technological innovation, Silicon Valley today has also earned itself a reputation as a hotbed of depression. That may be an unfortunate side effect of the relentless tech culture, but also another reason that microdosing may be gaining so much popularity, due to its effectiveness in mitigating depression and anxiety for some practitioners.

From Silicon Valley to the Collective Consciousness

The benefits of psychedelics as performance enhancers go beyond the labs and offices of Silicon Valley. Lore from extreme sport culture in the '60s and '70s is rife with stories of people using LSD to get the most from their bodies and minds. Psychedelics were a natural fit with extreme sport competitors – many of whom were veterans of the hippy movement of the '60s – who often saw themselves as rebels or outlaws.

"LSD can increase your reflex time to lightning speed, improve your balance to the point of perfection, increase your concentration . . . and make you impervious to weakness or pain," writer James Oroc claimed in a report for the Multidisciplinary Association for Psychedelic Studies.[xciv] "Various experienced individuals have climbed some of the hardest big walls in Yosemite, heli-skied first descents off Alaskan peaks, competed in world-class snowboarding competitions, raced motocross bikes, surfed enormous Hawaiian waves, flown hang-gliders above 18,00 feet, or climbed remote peaks in the Rockies, the Alps, the Andes, and even above 8,000 meters in the Himalayas–all while under the influence of LSD."

In a more conventional setting, Pittsburgh Pirates pitcher Dock Ellis famously claimed that he was on LSD when he threw a no-hitter in 1970. And outside of sports, countless bands and musicians, including the Beatles, Rolling Stones, Grateful Dead, Jefferson Airplane, and many more, cited LSD and other psychedelics for helping spark their creativity to write and perform music.

As general awareness of psychedelics expands, microdosing provides a palatable way for people who might be opposed to psychoactive reactions and hallucinations to consider the other benefits offered by substances such as LSD, mescaline, psilocybin, and ayahuasca. Framing their use as a tool to access flow states provides another way to combat the stigma that has long been attached to psychedelics in the United States.

All told, there are very few people in America or other developed countries who could say they haven't consumed media, used a piece of software, or watched an athletic performance that has been influenced by psychedelics. And now, the reach of these substances is spreading even further.

In addition to his attention-grabbing comments about billionaires, Tim Ferriss has been an active proponent of the benefits that psychedelics could bring to nearly any user who is open to their effects. Following one podcast on how psychedelics could be at the forefront of the next big medical breakthrough,[xcv] he hosted another show that looked specifically at microdosing. On that episode, he interviewed James Fadiman, the trailblazer in microdosing research. "[People who microdose] can be creative longer," Fadiman told Ferriss. "Kind of steady, more in flow."[xcvi]

Joe Rogan, a comedian and popular podcast host, has dedicated a number of episodes to exploring the experiences and breakthroughs that his guests have experienced using psychedelics. On one episode he talks specifically about microdosing with author and ethnopharmacologist Dennis McKenna, brother of renowned psychedelic explorer Terence McKenna.[xcvii] "People are using psilocybin these days in what they call microdosing, taking very small doses and seeing these profound benefits," Rogan says.

He speaks of his friend who takes doses before kickboxing and claims he can see things before they happen in the ring. "It's almost like he's reading people's minds before they're about to do something," says Rogan.

McKenna replies that he's not surprised at all. "[Psilocybin] is a lens through which you can look at the world and see aspects of it that are always there, but you've never noticed it before, because we're programmed not to," he explains. "They can reverse this background foreground relationship that we're so used to. Suddenly what's right in front of you is not so important and you can pay attention to the things in the background that you're programmed to suppress and ignore."

"They teach different ways of perception," McKenna continues. "You realize there's a different way to be in the world. There's a different way to perceive what you experience that normally you don't."

If the recent interest in microdosing originated in Silicon Valley, the phenomenon is rapidly spreading out around the globe, with potentially profound implications for the trajectory of humanity.

Psychedelics Help to Tap True Potential

Some experts argue that the increase in psychedelic use will lead human beings to conquer completely new horizons.

The book *Stealing Fire: How Silicon Valley, the Navy SEALs, and Maverick Scientists Are Revolutionizing the Way We Live and Work* by Steven Kotler and Jamie Wheal provides more evidence of how psychedelics help Silicon Valley entrepreneurs and others tap into their true potential, while grounding the subject in a historical context.[xcviii]

"As far back as we can trace Western civilization, buried among the stories that bore schoolchildren to tears, we find tales of rebel upstarts willing to bet it all for an altered state of consciousness," the authors write.

Today, as more people explore ways of altering their consciousness, the possibilities of what we can create expand to a dramatic degree. "We are witnessing a groundswell, a growing movement to storm heaven and steal fire," the book states. "It's a revolution in human possibility."

Altering our connection with the ego, be it through psychedelics, meditation, trances, virtual reality, or other means, we free the body and spirit to develop new and different ideas outside the framework in which humans often limit their thinking on a particular issue or problem. "When we consistently see more of 'what is really happening,' we can liberate ourselves from the limitations of our psychology," the authors say. "We can put our egos to better use, using them to modulate our neurobiology and with it, our experience. We can train our brains to find our minds."

"With our self forever standing guard over our ideas, crazy schemes and hare-brained notions tend to get filtered out long before they can become useful," *Stealing Fire* continues. "But intoxication lessens those constraints."

Silicon Valley, of course, makes a prime testing ground for crazy schemes and hare-brained notions. The combination of the limitless potential of technology with human beings pushing themselves beyond their own normal peripheries, through microdosing and other techniques, opens the door to boundless possibilities for our future.

---

lxxxvii

http://money.cnn.com/2015/01/25/technology/lsd-psychedelics-silicon-valley/
lxxxviii

http://money.cnn.com/2015/01/25/technology/lsd-psychedelics-silicon-valley/
lxxxix

https://www.1843magazine.com/features/turn-on-tune-in-drop-by-the-office
xc

https://www.amazon.com/What-Dormouse-Said-Counterculture-Personal/dp/0143036769
xci

https://www.theguardian.com/commentisfree/2011/sep/06/psychedelics-computer-revolution-lsd
xcii

https://www.recode.net/2014/4/3/11625260/at-hbos-silicon-valley-premiere-elon-musk-is-pissed
xciii

https://techcrunch.com/2013/05/15/google-ceo-larry-page-takes-the-stage-at-ceo-to-wrap-up-the-io-keynote/
xciv

http://www.maps.org/news-letters/v21n1/v21n1-25to29.pdf
xcv

http://tim.blog/2015/09/14/are-psychedelic-drugs-the-next-medical-breakthrough/

xcvi

http://tim.blog/2015/03/21/james-fadiman/
xcvii

https://www.youtube.com/watch?v=pUWaZ_wxhhg
xcviii

https://www.amazon.com/Stealing-Fire-Maverick-Scientists-Revolutionizing-ebook/dp/B01GCCT3G6/ref=sr_1_1?ie=UTF8&qid=1489749070&sr=8-1&keywords=stealing+fire+steven+kotler

Part II: How to Optimize Your Microdosing

Chapter 7: What is Legal and Illegal When Sourcing?

Sourcing the real thing – be it LSD or psilocybin – is the safest, most reliable way to start microdosing. In fact, according to the neuropsychopharmacologist David Nutt, LSD and psilocybin are among the least dangerous drugs in existence. Of course, in many countries they're also illegal, and this poses an obvious problem for microdosers.

At The Third Wave, we're often asked our advice on how to source materials for microdosing. The trouble for many is they lack an organic community from which to solicit psychedelics. Either they've never tried them before or, if they have, they've lost contact with their original suppliers.

Despite our enthusiasm for microdosing, many of us are left to our own devices when it comes to sourcing the substances.

In this chapter, we'll delve into some of the available options. But first, a couple of disclaimers:

- Despite the liberalization of cannabis laws (at least in the U.S.) and the conversation around drugs in general, you may still face heavy fines and incarceration for the possession of LSD or psilocybin. The same goes for many of the other substances used for microdosing, including mescaline, iboga, and ayahuasca. In other words, you undertake these experiments at your own risk, and we therefore recommend you take the time to personally research the possible legal consequences.

- Although the safety of LSD and psilocybin are well documented, far less is known (at least scientifically) about the safety of mescaline, iboga, ayahuasca, and other psychedelics. Certainly many of the "research chemicals" and "legal highs" (substances whose chemical formulas have been altered so that they're no longer illegal) that sometimes substitute for these psychedelics can be risky because they haven't been properly investigated. As always, the responsibility for weighing the potential benefits and harms of illicit substances is yours alone.

That said, we've endeavored to compile this chapter based on credible, up-to-date information.

Option 1: Find the Others

There's no shortage of the classical psychedelics LSD and psilocybin. And burgeoning interest in psychonautic research has fueled the supply of less known entheogens like iboga. You just need to know the right people.

So whenever someone asks me how to get hold of "real" substances for microdosing, I always give the same answer: Start building relationships.

Of course, this is easier said than done. But when I say build relationships, I don't necessarily mean with drug dealers. Unfortunately, decades of ill-advised prohibition have placed some of our most valuable and transformative tools into some pretty unsavory hands. This isn't to say that all suppliers are "drug dealers," or that all drug dealers engage in other criminal activities, but the risks and potential for ethical conflicts remain.

Fortunately, the mainstreaming of psychedelics has led to another exciting development: the resurgence of psychedelic societies. These above ground psychedelic communities are all about forging connections and building relationships.

Crucially, they're also about challenging stigma. Attracting members from wildly different backgrounds over a shared fascination with psychedelics, psychedelic societies have the potential to finally legitimize the field.

While none of these groups actually supply psychedelics to members, they're all invaluable forums for building connections and sharing experiences – not to mention integrating them.

Here's how to get involved:

1. Do an Internet search to find a psychedelic society near you.

2. Get in touch with your local society's leader.

3. Go to an event and start making connections.

You'll get more out of this if you go in the spirit of authentic community building. However, by co-creating these networks and helping to legitimize psychedelics, you'll inevitably come across the substances you seek.

Option 2: Use legal alternatives

Obviously depending on where you live, you may be able to find legal substitutes for both psilocybin mushrooms and LSD.

Psilocybin truffles
In the Netherlands, where psilocybin mushrooms have been illegal since 2008, it's still legal to buy psilocybin truffles, since they're not technically classed as "mushrooms."

Of course, this isn't much good if you don't live in the Netherlands – at least not at first glance. However, many legitimate suppliers based in the Netherlands routinely ship psilocybin truffles abroad. And even in the UK. where non-medical "psychoactive substances" are uniformly banned, authorities consider such imports a relatively low priority for law enforcement.

While buying truffles online is still a punishable crime in most countries, and not without its risk, it's an attractive option for many.

Alternatively, if you live in one of the Schengen Area (EU open borders zone) countries, and especially if you're close to the Netherlands, you could feasibly buy truffles in person and return home overland to avoid the risk of detection.

4-ACO-DMT

4-ACO-DMT is a synthetic tryptamine with structural similarities to psilocybin and psilocin. Doses as low as 2-3 mg can increase empathy and introspection, lift dark moods, and enhance visual perception. While some find microdoses a little too sedative for productivity at work, others find 4-ACO-DMT makes them more alert.

Either way, you're more or less free to experiment for yourself – unless you live in the U.K., Italy, Sweden, Belgium, or Brazil.

1P-LSD

1P-LSD (1-propionyl-lysergic acid diethylamide) is a semi-synthetic analog of LSD. In other words, it's closely related both structurally and chemically to lysergic acid diethylamide. According to some, it may only differ in absorption rate, duration, metabolism, and excretion. In fact, it may even be a "prodrug," converted to LSD by the body. Little is known for certain, but the effects by dosage of 1P-LSD are remarkably close to its relative.

And, for now at least, it's legal to buy in most European countries, the U.S., and Canada. If you're caught with it in some countries, including the U.S. (although it's not federally scheduled), 1P-LSD may be viewed as an (illegal) analog of an illegal substance. But it's widely available online. Check this list for possible vendors: https://www.reddit.com/r/RCSources/wiki/vendors.

Other LSD analogs

Numerous other "research chemical" analogs of LSD offer comparable dosage and effect profiles. They include AL-LAD, ALD-52, ETH-LAD, PRO-LAD, and LSZ.

Anecdotal reports list alertness, clarity, mood enhancement, and cognitive elasticity among their effects when microdosed. Some users even prefer these analogs to LSD.

In some countries, however, their legal status can be iffy. As with 1P-LSD, possession in the U.S. may or may not be prosecuted under the Federal Analogue Act; the law itself is ambiguously worded and case law is limited.[xcix-c] They also tend to be illegal in countries that take a more proactively suppressive approach to new drugs, including the UK., Latvia, Sweden, and Switzerland.

Ergoloid mesylates (Hydergine)

Developed by Albert Hofmann and marketed without FDA approval as a neuroprotective "smart drug," ergoloid mesylates is reportedly comparable at standard doses to microdoses of LSD.

It's only available on prescription in most Western countries, but you may be able to buy it online elsewhere.

2C-B-FLY

Active even at sub-milligram doses, the effects of 2C-B-FLY have been likened to mescaline and MDA (MDMA's more potent, more psychedelic predecessor). Microdoses of less than 100 μg (0.1 mg) may enhance motivation, empathy, creativity, and philosophical or abstract thinking.

2C-B-FLY is unscheduled in the U.S. but may be considered an illegal analog of 2C-B. In Canada, it's a Schedule III substance.

In any case, it's widely available online.

Amanita muscaria

Amanita muscaria – also known as the fly agaric mushroom – is completely legal in most countries. Notable exceptions include Australia, the Netherlands, and the UK.

Amanitas contain muscimol and ibotenic acid (not psilocybin and psilocin), so their effects differ from traditional psilocybin mushrooms – at least at macrodoses. Microdoses of 0.1-0.5 g have been found to relieve anxiety, enhance mood, increase energy, and generally impart a sense of "magic" to the world through insights and synchronicities.

Option 3: Grow your own

LSD is too complex (and legally risky) for most people to synthesize at home. But other substances for microdosing are pretty easy to cultivate.

Psilocybin
Although psilocybin mushrooms are banned in most countries, the spores are often legal. That means you can start growing your own for a consistent private supply. Home cultivation also minimizes the risk of misidentifying mushrooms in the wild.

For complete instructions, check out our "How to Grow Psilocybin Mushrooms" guide: https://thethirdwave.co/grow-psilocybin-mushrooms/.

Ergine (LSA)
Ergine, or lysergic acid amide (LSA), is structurally similar to LSD with vaguely comparable effects. Users tend to find it more sedating, often nauseating, and generally less potent than LSD. However, at microdoses, it can boost mental clarity and focus while relieving anxiety and depression.

It's also naturally occurring and, while the compound itself is widely illegal, ergine-containing seeds are not. Morning glories and Hawaiian baby woodrose are among the best known plant sources, and both are legal to grow in the U.S. (except Arizona), the UK., and mainland Europe (except Italy).

Common microdoses fall in the range of 5-15 morning glory seeds or 0.33-3 Hawaiian baby woodrose seeds. Usually, they're chewed for about 20 minutes and held under the tongue to absorb the ergine sublingually.

Mescaline
Cacti are well known as some of the easiest plants to grow, practically taking

care of themselves given the right conditions. And mescaline-containing cacti, such as peyote and San Pedro, are legal in most countries.

Although peyote cultivation is restricted in the U.S. to members of the Native American Church (or Peyote Religion), San Pedro can freely be grown for ornamental purposes.

Ibogaine

Iboga, including the whole plant and seeds, is illegal in the U.S. It's also restricted in a small number of European countries, as well as Australia and Canada, but seeds are widely available for shipping elsewhere.

Although adapted for the humid conditions of West African rainforests, iboga can adjust to drier climates – as long as temperatures remain well above 59 °F.

Ayahuasca

Plants used in traditional ayahuasca brews – including Banisteriopsis caapi and Psychotria viridis – are also adapted for the rainforest, so they need plenty of heat and moisture. They may need to be grown indoors. They can also take months or years to mature.

B. caapi delivers MAOIs and is used to ensure that the DMT in P. viridis is not broken down by the body. Both plants are legal in many countries, even if their alkaloids are not. But there are plenty of alternatives to choose from. These include Syrian rue, passion flower, and yohimbe for the MAOIs, and Mimosa hostilis, chaliponga, and reed canary grass for the DMT.

Your personal identity

Keep in mind that nothing can truly guarantee your anonymity online. Proxy networks and cryptocurrencies are only ways to mitigate the risk. Assuming your seller is genuine, they could still be hacked by law enforcement.

In June 2017, for instance, Dutch authorities seized Hansa, one of the largest darknet marketplaces. However, instead of shutting it down they continued to run it as normal, secretly collecting user data and transaction details. Meanwhile, the FBI shut down AlphaBay, another major marketplace, to funnel its users toward Hansa. Ultimately, Europol gathered 10,000 postal addresses and made numerous arrests.

While you're unlikely to be chased for buying a few tabs of acid or a small amount of psilocybin (even if they're seized in the mail) your details could still be logged.

Whichever route you choose, stay safe.

---

xcix

Yandiel Muniz, "Designer Drugs and the Federal Analog Act," *FIU Law Review*, https://law.fiu.edu/designer-drugs-federal-analog-act/
c

"Introduction to the Federal Controlled Substances Analogue Act," *Erowid*, January, 2001, https://www.erowid.org/psychoactives/law/analog/analog_info1.shtml

Chapter 8: How to Prepare a Microdose

So you've sourced a substance and you're ready to start microdosing. In the next chapter, we'll look at some protocols (i.e. how and when to take your microdoses) but first, some words on preparing them.

LSD

The most obvious way to microdose a paper tab (also known as a blotter) of LSD is to cut it up and take it in pieces. This is actually a fairly common method, but it's far from ideal for a number of reasons:

Reason #1: Your LSD may not be laid evenly.

During manufacture, blotter sheets of individual tabs are soaked in a liquid LSD solution and dried. However, this drying process is sometimes uneven. As a result, some parts of the paper are more concentrated than others. And because we're so sensitive to the molecule – and because we use such small amounts for microdosing – even the tiniest variations in potency can make all the difference.

Reason #2: Tabs are miniscule to begin with.

The standard size of a tab is a quarter-inch squared, so you might struggle to cut 10 or more equal pieces.

Reason #3: You risk wasting the chemical.

The longer you spend handling tabs, exposing them to light, air, and heat – as well as moisture if you're not wearing gloves – the more likely you are to degrade your LSD.

In short, it's just not worth the hassle, especially when there's a far more effective, and much easier, method available.

Volumetric microdosing ensures consistency by dissolving your tab's LSD content in a sterile liquid solution. All you need is a small bottle, a 1 ml syringe (with a blunt needle), and some distilled water or vodka.

Follow these steps to get started:

1. Prepare your container

If you have a dark glass bottle or something opaque for your solution, you just need to make sure that it's clean. If your bottle is clear, on the other hand, you'll have to shield its contents from light damage. Tin foil works fine.

2. Fill it with vodka or distilled water

For a standard 100-microgram (μg) tab, it keeps things simple to use 10 ml of solvent. This way, 1 ml of your solution should contain exactly 10 μg of LSD, and you can reliably adjust this dose up and down by the graduations on your syringe.

Alternatively, you may choose to use a shop-bought miniature (50 ml) bottle of vodka. You'll need to consume more alcohol for the same dose, but it won't be enough to get tipsy.

If you're using water, make absolutely sure it's distilled because the chlorine in tap water destroys LSD upon contact. For this reason, you should also avoid consuming tap water, or brushing your teeth with it, for at least one hour before and after you microdose.

3. Add LSD

Drop one tab of acid into your vodka or water and secure the lid. Then shake it and store it in a cool, dark place. A fridge is ideal, but if it's shared you'll probably want to label the bottle. Otherwise, anywhere out of heat and light is fine. Leave the solution for 24 hours or so before you use it. The tab itself won't dissolve, but it's fine to leave in the bottle if you've used vodka. If you've used distilled water, though, you should fish it out with tweezers to minimize the risk of contamination.

Your solution should last at least a few months, and probably longer if you've used vodka.

4. Measure your first microdose

Obviously it helps to know the dose on your tabs, but that's not always possible. So if you don't know for certain, just assume that each one contains 100 μg of acid. Divide this number by the volume (ml) of your solution to calculate how many micrograms of LSD are in each milliliter.

The standard microdose falls between 10 and 20 μg, so if you have 10 ml of solution you'll need between 1 and 2 (1 ml) syringes' worth for a dose. If you've used 50 ml, you'll need 5-10 syringes' worth for a dose (or a bigger syringe!).

Psilocybin

As with LSD, it's tempting to cut up psilocybin mushrooms and take little bits as your microdoses. Again, however, this won't ensure consistency. That's because the amount of psilocybin differs not only between strains, but also between individual mushrooms within the same strain – and even between the caps and stems of the same mushrooms. Potency often depends more on maturity and growing conditions than it does on size. In fact, immature "pins" may contain more psilocybin than older, fully grown mushrooms.

The best way to ensure a consistent microdose is to:

- Choose a strain and stick to it.

It's fine to experiment, of course, but you may have to start over with a low-end microdose each time you try a new strain. It's a lot easier and far more reliable just to pick a strain and keep it.

- Grind your (dried) psilocybin mushrooms.

This should result in a fine powder with an even distribution of psilocybin – perfect for microdosing. For this, you'll need a set of digital scales (accurate to at least 0.1 g, or 100 mg), a food dehydrator or desiccant, and a coffee grinder.

Here's how to get started:

1. Dry your mushrooms

There are several different methods for drying mushrooms, ranging in price and efficiency. The quickest and most dependable, but also the most expensive at around $40, is to use a food dehydrator. This will get your mushrooms "cracker dry," that is, they'll snap when you try to bend them, which is exactly what you want for grinding. Another method is to air dry your mushrooms with a fan and then place them in an airtight container with (but not touching) a desiccant. This takes longer but it's cheap and effective.

2. Grind them up.

Weigh out enough of your dried mushrooms for the amount and size of the microdoses you want to prepare. On average, microdoses range between 200 and 500 mg. So if you're new to microdosing, and especially if you're new to psilocybin, you may want to start with 4 grams for 20 microdoses of 200 mg each. Of course, you can always increase your dose by taking more as you go along.

Next, place your dried mushrooms into a coffee grinder and pulse for up to a minute. Be sure to allow time for the particles to settle, since if you open the chamber too soon you may lose a lot of the powder. It's also advisable to use a different coffee grinder than the one you normally use for your coffee, as the blades can be hard to clean. I'm assuming you don't want psychedelic residue in your coffee from now on – not least because of the earthy taste.

3. Transfer the powder for storage and microdosing.

Many people use a capsule machine or homemade tamping rod to transfer the powder to capsules. If you go this route, start with the "Size 3" capsules, since these hold about 200 mg depending on how you pack them.

Alternatively, you could transfer all of your powder to a Mason jar for storage and weigh out as much as you need each time you want a microdose – adding it to juice, honey, or cereal as desired. The downside to this method is repeated exposure to air and potential condensation whenever you open the jar. But you should be all right if you don't grind too much at a time – perhaps enough for a couple of weeks at the most.

Whichever method you choose, psilocybin will last longest in the freezer. You just have to make sure that it's in an airtight container, ideally with a silica gel packet.

Ayahuasca

As I mentioned in the previous chapter, you can legally buy or grow the ingredients you need to make ayahuasca at home. Actually, without the support of a shaman, what you're really making is a kind of ayahuasca analog.

For the classic ayahuasca analog recipe, which yields one standard dose for maybe 10 microdoses, you'll need:

- 25 g Psychotria viridis leaves, dried and ground (alt: 9 g Mimosa hostilis or 20 g Acacia)
- 3 g Peganum harmala seeds, crushed (alt: 4-5 g Syrian rue seeds or 50-60 g Banisteriopsis caapi leaves)
- Juice of one lemon
- Water

Follow these steps to brew it:

1. Place all of your ingredients in a pot and bring to the boil. Continue to boil for 2-3 minutes, then reduce the heat and simmer for 5 minutes.

2. Pour the liquid (your first decoction) into a separate container, leaving behind the plant material.

3. Add more water to the cooking pot and bring to the boil again.

4. Return the first decoction to the pot. After a few minutes, pour all of the liquid into the separate container and repeat step 3.

5. Strain this fresh brew into the first/second decoctions and discard the plant material.

6. Finally, return all of the liquid to the pot and simmer to reduce in volume.

7. Allow to cool.

98

You'll need to experiment to find the right microdose for you. For example, you could start with one tenth of the standard ayahuasca dose and roll it back next time if it's too intense or noticeably psychedelic.

When you've found the right level, freeze your brews in microdose portions for long-term storage and thaw them out for use.

Iboga

When microdosing iboga, many people just consume the root bark. 1 g appears to be a good starting point. An alternative method is to grind it and fill capsules with up to 500 mg each.

As with LSD and psilocybin, however, the concentration of the primary psychoactive compound (in this case ibogaine) varies. Extracts are therefore widely preferred, not only for consistency between doses, but for economical potency as well.

Although illegal in several countries, including the U.S. (but curiously not the UK.), iboga extracts can be purchased online. Most users prefer the concentrated total alkaloid (TA) tincture, of which just one drop is usually enough for a microdose. The TA extract is also available in powder form. You may need 50-100 mg of this, which you can swallow in a capsule or stir into liquid.

Alternatively, you may wish to start with a 25 mg dose of an isolated ibogaine HCl extract. It offers a shallower experience according to some, but it's a purer form of the primary psychoactive alkaloid.

Mescaline

Mescaline, like ibogaine, is just one of the alkaloids present in peyote, torch cactus, and several other cacti. And again the concentrations vary. But if you can't find extracted mescaline and you don't want to extract it yourself,[ci] eating the raw material is fine. In fact, various Native American groups are known to "microdose" peyote while hunting to improve their stamina.

Take some time to experiment for yourself to find the right dosage. Half of one mid-sized peyote button or 1-2 one-inch slices of a torch cactus like San Pedro would make a good start.

Moving forward

Now that we've covered how to prepare your microdose, we'll take a look at microdosing protocols – how frequently to do it, when not to, and practical advice for optimizing your microdosing experience.

[ci]

Adam Gottlieb, *Peyote and Other Psychoactive Cacti* (Berkeley, CA: Ronin Publishing, 1977)

Chapter 9: Protocols for Microdosing

As microdosers, essentially, we're carrying out experiments on ourselves – and, as Jim Fadiman has pointed out, in largely uncharted territory. It's therefore useful to have some kind of procedural constraints, or protocols, not only to guide us but to minimize harm as well.

The protocol we use is Fadiman's, which he developed based on early reports from self-study participants. The routine is to take one microdose, in the morning, on Day 1 and Day 4 of each cycle, or week. So, if you take your first microdose on a Sunday,[cii] you'll take your second on a Wednesday, spending the other days of the week recovering and observing the residual effects.

Throughout each cycle, you should keep notes on the effects of each dose – things like your mental state, emotions, behavior, and so on – while following your normal routine.

Fadiman recommends an initial term of 10 cycles, after which some people stop microdosing and others, more commonly, continue to microdose on an ad hoc basis when they feel like it. Because we don't yet know enough about the long-term effects of microdosing, it might not be wise to jump straight into more cycles – although many do.

Tolerance

Unlike other drugs, psychedelics have little to no long-term tolerance. As long as your psychedelic intake is spaced out by 48 hours, then there will be little to no difference in your tolerance.

This makes for a tricky dilemma when microdosing. After all, if you microdose for a while and notice the benefits, you may be tempted to microdose daily.

The fact is, not a great deal is known about the possible buildup of tolerance when microdosing. Some people experience no tolerance effect whatsoever from daily microdoses, while others find the effects diminished. Some appear to be more sensitive than others. Indeed, a number of people even claim that the best way to benefit from microdosing is to space each dose as much as two weeks apart!

In any case, the question of tolerance may be moot. Fadiman's research protocol is primarily designed to collect meaningful (i.e. standardized) data from a large sample, deliberately returning participants to baseline consciousness as an experimental control. Basically, if you microdose too often you run the risk of having a limited frame of reference for gauging how you're affected.

Also, as Fadiman points out, the residual effects of LSD at standard doses last weeks, not just the 12 or so hours of the trip itself. In the same way, the residual effects of microdosing can last up to two days. That means you're probably wasting your supply if you use it daily.[ciii]

Other protocols

Fadiman's basic protocol is an ideal framework for starting out. But depending on your specific reasons for microdosing (see the Chapter 3 section about intentions), you may wish to add further, more specialized protocols that better serve your aims. To this end, we've developed a number of suggestions.

Anxiety
If you've ever suffered from anxiety, you'll know the importance of getting the right amount of sleep. When microdosing, you need to be even more vigilant – particularly with LSD, since its relatively long duration could potentially disrupt your sleeping pattern.

The best advice, whatever substance you're using, is to microdose as early in the day as possible – ideally before 10:00 AM. In general, you should aim to microdose at least 12 hours before you go to bed. Integrating meditation and regular exercise into your microdosing protocol is also highly recommended.

If you find that microdosing actually seems to increase your anxiety, as some do, you may want to try the following:

- Remember that psychedelics are a tool for increasing patience and compassion including toward yourself. Observe these traits above all others and reinforce them through journaling. In this way, you'll be able to strengthen and promote the developing neural pathways that underpin them.
- Use deep breathing[civ] exercises to physically detach yourself from anxious thoughts. "Box breathing" is a good example. Simply breathe in for a count of four, hold in for four, breathe out for four, hold out for four, and start the process again for a total of four repetitions.
- Spend time in nature and away from modern technology. Make this a regular part of your protocol. If you can incorporate exercise and meditation, even better!

Generalized anxiety disorder

Obviously anxiety isn't always manageable in the usual ways. Often, it can be extremely persistent, manifesting without identifiable cause as generalized anxiety disorder. In this case – at least according to Fadiman and Korb's research – microdosing could potentially exacerbate your symptoms, possibly by increasing your awareness of the underlying causes.

That doesn't mean you should avoid it altogether, only that you may want to proceed with caution. In fact, preparing for subconscious issues to surface while microdosing could make them easier to deal with. Ultimately, you should view microdosing as an opportunity to work through these blind spots, organizing yourself and your surroundings accordingly.

Of course, if you do feel that microdosing worsens your symptoms without doing anything to help them long-term, you should probably lower your dose or stop it entirely. Microdosing isn't for everyone, at least not right away. You may want to return to it later, perhaps after you've had more success with other approaches like meditation, exercise, and prioritizing quality sleep.

Social anxiety

Social anxiety, on the other hand, appears to benefit in almost all cases from microdosing. Many have enthused in particular about feeling less "in their head" and more "in the moment," which is crucial for what essentially boils down to a fear of negative judgment.

You may want to take things slowly at first, though. For example, you could start by microdosing around the people you're closest to, then, as an experimental protocol, expand to other situations you found uncomfortable before.

Depression

According to anecdotal reports, microdosing works wonders for depression. We dug into why this is the case in Chapter 5, the Science of Microdosing. However, it's best not to think of it as a magic pill. In fact, many find themselves slipping back into old, depressive mindsets after they stop.

That's why it's crucial to spend your microdosing time making positive changes to outlast the protocol itself. This could mean adopting new habits that support your mental health, including better nutrition, regular meditation, and exercise. Setting aside some time each day to think about what you're grateful for (not forgetting yourself) is another useful trick. It might sound hokey, but the benefits of inward gratitude are consistently backed by research.[cv]

ADD/ADHD

If you're microdosing with the goal of replacing ADD/ADHD medications like Adderall, Vyvanse, or Ritalin, expect the effects to be subtler and more gradual than you're used to. They'll also be less frequent if you're following Jim Fadiman's protocol.

Taking your regular course of treatment while microdosing isn't recommended, because the increased heart strain and mental "speediness" may detract from the benefits – not to mention your health. On the other hand, stopping cold turkey may also be problematic. Instead, try to wean off slowly over the course of the entire protocol. And seriously consider running plans past your physician.

If you tend to be self-critical, like many with ADD/ADHD, you could make this a focus of your journal. Recording changes in your self-image can help to strengthen and reinforce new perspectives as they develop.

Another good protocol to follow, particularly if you're given to impulsivity (a trait amplified by microdosing) is to refrain from major decisions while under the immediate effects. We'll delve into this in more detail in the following chapter.

Personal growth

Of course, you might not be looking to "solve" anything by microdosing. You may just be curious to find out how the practice deepens your own personal development and growth. If this is the case, you're likely to benefit from extended breaks between each run of 10 cycles (at least if you plan to repeat the protocol) so as not to become psychologically dependent on microdosing.

One central tenet of any personal development program – microdosing or not – is cultivating intention in the transformation you want to see. To ensure your own accelerated evolution through the avenue of microdosing, set significant time aside before beginning a protocol to think through a few questions:

- If you could choose only one thing to do better next month, what would you choose?
- What type of connections would you like to make with others?

- Think of someone who you admire. What qualities and virtues do they possess that you would like to practice this month?

These are just a sample of the many questions we include in our Microdosing Workbook, included in our extensive online microdosing course.

Finally, you may also want to ask those you're close to for feedback. Oftentimes, we don't have clear insight on how we have changed as a result of microdosing. If you have a spouse or partner, or spend significant time with a group of friends, ask them to comment on changes they notice while you are microdosing. Integrate this feedback – positive or constructive – when reflecting on how microdosing has helped accelerate your own path of personal development.

Creativity

If you're specifically interested in microdosing for creativity, you might like to try a mini or museum dose. Mini-dosing is slightly perceptible. If microdosing LSD is approximately 15 micrograms for you, then a mini-dose may be closer to 25-30 micrograms. Museum dose would be closer to 50 micrograms.

Generally speaking, the higher the dose, the more divergent your thinking – which is basically what creativity is: thinking that is abstract or non-linear.

Inevitably, of course, there comes a point on any psychedelic where your thinking becomes so divergent that you lose the ability or will to *create*. However, doses that fall somewhere between a microdose and a full trip (again, mini-dose or museum dose) have proved beneficial for many in the creative and conceptualization process.

One important note about facilitating creative insight with microdosing: it is critical not to strictly rely on the substance to engender creative insight. As we've emphasized throughout this book, the environment in which you micro or mini dose is just as important as the substance itself.

If micro or mini-dosing for creative purposes, I've found two avenues to be best for the conceptualization process:

- Spending time in nature with close friends and/or business partners
- Spending time along with a journal and pen and letting your mind wander (think brainstorming on psychedelics)

Minimizing distractions and creating a space to let your mind wander and go deep into conceptualization will make the creative process much easier.

Leadership

Many have found microdosing to be an excellent tool in the development of modern leadership skills. We'll look more closely at this in Chapter 11, but if this is your focus then it's crucial to observe not only your behavior, but the ways in which people react to you.

You should also be wary of impulsivity. Take care to implement protocols that ensure responsible decision-making, such as postponing decisions until the second day after a microdose.

Above all, keep in mind that your role as a leader is to nurture, not dominate, others. The idea is to attract people to your vision, not coerce them into it. Try to cultivate a strong habit of reflexivity in your journaling and day-to-day interactions.

Paul Stamets's Protocol

Paul Stamets is the world's leading authority on the medicinal and environmental use of mushrooms, including psilocybin mushrooms.

In November 2017, Paul appeared on the Joe Rogan podcast, where he spoke about a slightly different protocol than Dr. Fadiman's.

Whereas Fadiman has recommended a 2x per week protocol – one day on two days off – Stamets's recommendation is five days on, two days off. Further, Stamets recommends combining it with additional medicinal mushrooms – like Lion's mane – for the synergistic effect.

In short, Stamets treats microdosing more like an ongoing supplement to consistently strengthen connectivity between neurological nodes and Fadiman treats microdosing more as a short-term intervention to help get people "unstuck" from specific medical conditions.

Magical protocols

Much of this chapter applies to virtually any substance for microdosing, but some people also devise protocols for using specific plant medicines. These tend to approach psychedelic substances with respect, either as spiritual sacraments or as beings in their own right – calling to mind the Bwiti reverence of iboga, the Quechua concept of ayahuasca, meaning "spirit vine," and the Huichol deification of Peyote.

Devising rituals based on traditional concepts in this way, particularly if you're impressed by such imagery, could potentiate the effects. One ibogaine microdoser, for example, recommends, "letting in the spirit of iboga" to manifest positive affirmations and intentions like "I am complete," "this day is perfect," "life is generous," or "my body is healing itself."[cvi]

You can learn all about plant medicines and their cultural significance from various sources, including The Third Wave website, as a basis for your own magical protocols.

[cii]

This is possibly ideal if you're a first-timer and you work weekdays, since you'll have the day off to comfortably test the immediate effects, as well as the following day to observe the residual effects in the workplace.

ciii

MAPS, "James Fadiman & Sophia Korb: Microdosing - The Phenomenon, Research Results & Startling Surprises," *YouTube*, April 26, 2017, https://www.youtube.com/watch?v=JBgKRyRCVFM

civ

Deep breathing means inhaling into the diaphragm, or the abdomen, rather than the chest.

cv

"In Praise of Gratitude," Harvard Mental Health Letter, November, 2011, https://www.health.harvard.edu/newsletter_article/in-praise-of-gratitude

cvi

Bancopuma, "Iboga Microdosing Guide," DMT-Nexus forum post, December 27, 2013, https://www.dmt-nexus.me/forum/default.aspx?g=posts&t=52279

Chapter 10: Microdosing for Creativity and Flow States

Proponents of microdosing say that taking regular, small quantities of psychedelics enhances their performance, whether for improving code or coming up with creative business solutions. The practice works by inducing flow states in users, a phrase coined by psychologist Mihaly Csikszentmihalyi as part of an investigation into optimal human experience.[cvii] In other words, the substances help people improve their focus on creative endeavors, with a dramatic effect on the ability to remain mindful. The description of "being in the zone" that many extreme sports participants attribute to LSD and other psychedelics also echoes the description of flow state given by Silicon Valley microdosing enthusiasts.

In practice, that means improved concentration and creativity, which can result in developing novel ideas to solve difficult problems – a perfect tool for a software entrepreneur, or anyone in a field that requires innovation or insight.

A freelancer wrote in to The Third Wave to describe the benefits of getting into a flow state: "While I was working on a project during the day I'm micro dosing, I used to give it much more effort and time and I was really enjoying what I'm doing without getting lost somewhere else or taking breaks from time to time, I was living at the moment without any distraction from outside. Yeah it made what I do more enjoyable."

As I've mentioned before, the most authoritative source of information about microdosing yet compiled is James Fadiman's book, *The Psychedelic Explorer's Guide.*[cviii] Fadiman provides suggested protocol for microdosing and has been collecting reports for several years about how psychedelics have affected his readers. "In low doses, they facilitate awareness of solutions to technical and artistic problems," he notes.

People who followed his protocol wrote to him about the ways in which microdosing improved their concentration. "Was able to shut out virtually all distracting influences," one report said.

"I was impressed with the intensity of concentration, the forcefulness and exuberance with which I could proceed toward the solution," another wrote.

A third user had a similar experience. "My experience during the session was an unbelievable increase in the ability to concentrate and make decisions. It was impossible to procrastinate. Cobwebs, blocks, and binds disappeared."

Fadiman's respondents reported increases in their creativity as well. "I've found that I've had some brilliant outbursts (at least they seemed brilliant to me) with respect to both work product and personal creative projects," one wrote in. "What seems to happen is that the 'flow' state described by Mihaly Csikszentmihalyi and noted frequently in the sports arena is a lot easier to access and stay in."

Other respondents said they found similar results. "Sub-doses of 10 to 20 micrograms allow me to increase my focus, open my heart, and achieve breakthrough results while remaining integrated within my routine," one reader said.

"I would venture to say that my wit, response time, and visual and mental acuity seem greater than normal on it," another wrote.

Third Wave readers also reported overall positive results. In one Third Wave survey, 25.5 percent of 51 respondents said they noticed improved problem solving after microdosing. In a second survey, 229 individuals ranked the results of microdosing on various aspects of their performance on a scale of 1 to 6. Respondents gave an average score of 4.65 for span of focus, 4.57 for problem solving, and 4.76 for creativity. For general mood, microdosers reported an average score of 5.2.

Not every person said that microdosing helped with focus or creativity, but many reported significant benefits. "I struggle with concentration and can be very irritable, micro dosing greatly improves that for me," a real estate agent and U.S. military veteran said in the survey. Another report, from a teacher in the Netherlands, stated, "at the end of the day a wow feeling of everything that was accomplished."

An actor described how microdosing provided an enhanced ability to be present in the craft: "Conversation flowed beautifully, like my mind always found the words I was looking for. It was great for my acting ability too, felt much more present during challenging scenes."

Several people described to The Third Wave the benefits that microdosing offered to their collaborative efforts in the workplace. "My positivity has sky rocketed, and I feel that I put out such a positive energy force that I attracted positive results in my workplace – such as getting new clients, treating my staff better, the list can truly go on," said one individual.

"I was no longer sensitive to criticism or confrontations, my work ethic improved and I was much more open and caring for customers and coworkers. It became less about me and more about the collective," another reported.

"[It was] easier to work with, collaborate with colleagues," a reader wrote in, "even those who've been difficult in the past; better able to concentrate and connect all day rather than in fits and starts; clarity in presenting and a general overall sense of understanding and being able to communicate complex ideas."

While the sheer volume of anecdotal evidence spread across so many venues is a testament to the results that the practice offers to many people – sometimes in world-changing ways – not everyone who tries microdosing reports a positive or useful effect on their work performance. Reporters for *Vox* and the Seattle-based newspaper *The Stranger* tried microdosing themselves.

"At one point during my first session, I looked up and realized I'd been totally engrossed in my work with no real awareness of anything else for an hour," Baynard Woods wrote in *Vox* after taking a tiny hit of LSD. "I found myself more deeply absorbed in that zone we all hope to be in where the doer and the deed dissolve together into the pleasure of pure work."[cix] But he had a difficult experience with night terrors after he mixed microdosing with heavy alcohol use.

Katie Herzog in *The Stranger* found a similar result. "It's not uncommon for me to spend more time wandering than writing," she wrote. "But on that particular day, I didn't wander at all, and by the time I looked up, it was dark. This continued into the next day when I wasn't microdosing, and I still got more done in an afternoon than I had the previous week."[cx] However, Herzog decided that despite the benefits to her work, LSD wasn't a solution for the anxiety she felt, so she turned to therapy.

Ultimately, both writers came off ambivalent about their experiments. Their reports are an important reminder that microdosing isn't a magic potion that will automatically bring success and happiness to everyone. Each individual must find his or her own path to what works and feels comfortable.

Studies on How Microdosing Can Help Creativity, Focus, and Problem Solving

As I've stated throughout this book, we do not have a comprehensive body of scientific research that backs up the wave of anecdotal reports about the benefits of microdosing. However, there are studies involving people taking full doses of psychedelics that corroborate the idea that the substances can improve creativity and problem solving, and give us hints as to why.

In 1966 Fadiman conducted research that involved giving 200 mg of mescaline sulphate to 27 subjects who worked mostly in the fields of science, math, and engineering.[cxi] He instructed each subject to focus on a tricky, unsolved professional problem they had been working on. After ingesting the mescaline, participants spent three hours relaxing, followed by an hour of tests, and then were given four hours to work on their problem.

The staff conducting the study gave several instructions to participants to help them home in on solutions. Subjects were told to try to identify the process at the center of the problem, and then scan through any number of possible solutions, trusting the brain to intuit the correct answer when it came across it. The staff reminded participants that they would be able to see a bigger picture of the problem, putting it in a new perspective, and that a break from their ego provided by the psychedelic would allow them to seek the best answers based on merit and not worry about saving face or salvaging previous approaches that didn't work out.

Nearly everyone who participated in the experiment reported that his or her problem-solving ability was enhanced. A dozen found that they had conceptualized solutions to their problems, some with deep real-world applications. Among the results: breakthroughs in ideas or products such as space probe experiments, electron accelerators, a conceptual photon design, brick and mortar building designs, medical diagnoses, and a vibratory microtome (a tool to create very thin slices of animal and plant tissues or other materials).

In their reports following the experiment, the subjects described 11 ways in which their experience enhanced their functioning. For some, the mescaline helped lower their inhibition or fear of failure. "Although doing well on these problems would be fine, failure to get ahead on them would be threatening. However, as it turned out, on this afternoon the normal blocks in the way of progress seemed to be absent," one of the participants said afterward.

Others said they were able to see their problems in a larger context, and also experienced an enhanced fluency and flexibility of ideation. "I could handle two or three different ideas at the same time and keep track of each," a subject claimed. "I also got the feeling that creativity is an active process in which you limit yourself and have an objective, so there is a focus about which ideas can cluster and relate," another said.

Study participants had a heightened capacity for visual imagery and fantasy, and also reported an increased ability to concentrate on their problem. "I was impressed with the intensity of concentration, the forcefulness and exuberance with which I could proceed toward the solution," one said.

Subjects also said they felt heightened empathy with external processes, helping them grasp the problem in its entirety and understand how objects and components function within it. They additionally reported an increased sense of empathy, further improving problem-solving capacity.

What's more, participants noted that subconscious data in their brains was more accessible, and they could associate dissimilar ideas to help come to a breakthrough. Finally, they said that they felt heightened motivation to obtain closure, and were able to visualize the completed solution. "I visualized the result I wanted and subsequently brought the variables into play which could bring that result about," one said. "I had great visual (mental) perceptibility; I could imagine what was wanted, needed, or not possible with almost no effort. I was amazed at my idealism, my visual perception, and the rapidity with which I could operate."

"The practical value of obtained solutions is a check against subjective reports of accomplishment that might be attributable to temporary euphoria," the experiment concludes. "We are dealing with materials and experimental situations that have long-term effects; it would be foolhardy and irresponsible to treat this kind of research as if it were isolated from the fabric of the subjects' lives."

In subsequent years, there have been few follow-up experiments due to federal prohibition on psychedelics and accompanying obstacles to scientific research. However, anecdotal reports that support its conclusion have surfaced from time to time.

In the book *LSD — The Problem-Solving Psychedelic*, P.G. Stafford and B.H. Golightly reveal the tale of a naval researcher who used LSD to develop a solution regarding the design of a submarine detection device.[cxii] He said after years of unsuccessfully working on the problem the idea took ten minutes to develop after he took the acid. His inspiration resulted in a patented device that was used by the Navy. The book goes on to describe advances in furniture design, visual arts, and writing experienced by people under the influence of LSD.

In another anecdotal look, researcher Jeremy Narby spoke with three molecular biologists after they took ayahuasca for the first time, and each one responded that they had come to insights that would be useful for their professional research.

Benny Shanon, a cognitive psychologist at The Hebrew University, described an unexpected outburst of creativity on the piano while using ayahuasca, writing "I played for more than an hour, and the manner of my playing was different from anything I have ever experienced. It was executed in one unfaltering flow, constituting an ongoing narration that was being composed as it was being executed. It appeared that my fingers just knew where to go."[cxiii]

More recently, researchers have been compiling information that helps us understand exactly how psychedelics can help improve human performance. A 2016 study by the Beckley Foundation, "Ayahuasca and Creativity: the Amazonian Plant Brew Improves Divergent Thinking," provides evidence that the psychedelic drink made from Amazonian jungle plants can help people with their problem solving abilities.[cxiv] The research looks at how the substance impacts users' ability to think divergently – or outside the box – to consider many different possible solutions to a situation or problem.

The study assessed 26 participants by having them identify associations between cartoon pictures of animals and everyday objects. The subjects were tested both before they took the ayahuasca, and about two hours after they drank it. After ingesting the drink, participants were able to come up with more alternative associations between the pictures, demonstrating an increase in divergent thinking.

The researchers suggested conducting a follow-up study that would also assess the subjects' mood, under the hypothesis that a positive mindset would correlate to an uptick in divergent thinking. They also recommended assessing the usefulness of the creative ideas generated under ayahuasca, and tracking the longevity of the effects on divergent thinking.

"It is important to bear in mind that psychedelics help us to make full use of our inborn creative capabilities, rather than . . . supplying us with additional creativity," the study's authors concluded.

In a similar vein, a University College London study suggested that LSD boosted the capacity for associative thinking. Subjects were asked to name objects they were shown, and many who had taken LSD erroneously misidentified the props by naming related things instead, for example saying "foot" when shown an image of a shoe.[cxv]

"This study suggests that LSD puts our brains in a state similar to that found in dreaming, where thoughts become less logical and more associative," an article in the *Psychedelic Scientist* notes. "The increase in connectivity produced in the brain by LSD is amazingly complex, and results in profound changes in cognition."[cxvi]

Third Wave readers also experienced the benefits of divergent thinking. "All topics become more interesting," a pharmacology student from Australia said. "Attention is increased and not lateral minded, as I subconsciously think of a problem from multiple angles."

"I felt like there was a click in my lens of perception. I thought about things from a different light, [a] different manner... all-around really enjoyable," reported another respondent to a Third Wave survey.

Both divergent and associative thinking could prove very useful indeed to scientists and engineers working on difficult problems that require insight from outside the usual framework that they use to approach the subject. Brain scans of people using LSD show that the chemical triggers activity all over the brain, allowing new pathways and connections to form, which could explain why psychedelics are so effective at lifting the restrictions of conventional thinking.[cxvii]

The sum of the research combined with anecdotal reports leads to the conclusion that humans do not function at full capacity unless there is a catalyst or instigator. By limiting the censors that govern conscious awareness, psychedelics can and do dramatically expand the possibilities of what human beings can accomplish, and microdosing is a promising way to advance toward that vision.

Contextualizing Microdosing within the Flow States Trend

I've already discussed my own experience with flow and how microdosing enabled me to overcome professional issues with procrastination and creative resistance. For the first time, I was able to execute consistently and to the level of excellence that I wanted, leading as I've said to The Third Wave.

In *Stealing Fire*, Steven Kotler and Jamie Wheal break flow states down into their component parts – selflessness (ego loss), timelessness (time dilation or contraction), effortlessness, and richness (vivid insights and detailed information) – taking a broader look at the mechanisms involved.[cxviii] By understanding their psychological and neurobiological basis, they argue, we can identify the best, most reliable means for their induction.

As they point out, the prevalence of psychoactive substances across a whole range of species – from birds to baboons to dolphins to elephants – suggests a basic evolutionary drive toward altered, disruptive, or de-patterning states of consciousness. However, psychedelics are far from the only means for attaining them.

Sensory deprivation tanks, in which people float on body-temperature saltwater in pitch-black darkness, are also found to enhance creativity, concentration, and coordination.[cxix] The elite Navy SEAL Team Six, or DEVGRU, actually uses them in training, outfitted with audiovisual inputs to cut the already intensive six month period of foreign language acquisition to just six weeks.[cxx]

Other flow state "technologies" are more ancient, but just as effective in ways we're beginning to understand.

Yoga, for instance (hatha yoga in particular), is all about harmonizing the body and mind. It systematically negates the notion of a mind-body split, and has been doing so since long before the emergence of "embodied cognition" as an academic field. As researchers like Guy Claxton now emphasize, the body is above all an interrelated system of systems. It's why physical movement reduces stress and how, more specifically, striking a dominant pose for just two minutes a day can up-regulate testosterone by 20 percent and down-regulate the stress hormone cortisol by 15 percent.[cxxi]

Similarly, when immersed in yogic movements, practitioners frequently experience a sense of energized focus, vibrancy, and peace – the flow state, or *dhyana* to use the yogic parlance. Patanjali's Yoga Sutra lays out specific instructions for attaining this state, first by *pratyahara* – withdrawing the senses, or ignoring distractions – then by *dharana* – focusing the senses on just one activity or movement.[cxxii]

We can draw obvious parallels here between yoga and other practices, extending not only to meditation but also to intense, ecstatic prayer. Returning to Kotler and Wheal's flow state components, these modalities appear to be especially effective at fostering the first, i.e. selflessness or ego loss. Brain imaging studies carried out by "neurotheologists" like Andrew Newberg have found, for instance, a deactivation of the right parietal lobe during moments of peak spiritual contemplation. This part of the brain is involved in navigation and the perception of distance, which in turn are based on our awareness of the body's physical boundaries. According to Newberg, this deactivation of the right parietal lobe occurs as part of the brain's diversion of energy toward focus. "When this happens, we can no longer distinguish self from other," he says.[cxxiii]

Some find the effects of meditation to be strikingly similar to microdosing, while others highlight key, perhaps complementary, differences. Whereas microdosing enhances energy, sharpness, action, and risk-taking, for example, meditation promotes calm equanimity, emotional grounding, and stillness. Most agree that the efficacy of both modalities at least partially depends on the mindset you bring into them, the optimum being a certain level of calmness to begin with.[cxxiv]

A note of caution: The idea that any one modality, such as microdosing, is inferior to another, such as meditation, simply because its mastery requires no repetition is not only elitist but actually pretty dangerous. This attitude tends to be prevalent among orthodox religious traditions that have refined and perfected techniques of ecstasy over centuries of practice.

Again, by studying the neurological mechanisms behind the ecstatic state of oneness or unity, a key component of flow states, we can separate the wheat from the chaff, so to speak. We can identify which aspects of traditional or mystical methodologies are truly necessary for attaining flow states and effectively use scientific data to refine religious praxis.

Rhythmic activities such as dancing, drumming, and sex have a similar effect on the brain, synchronizing and channeling neural activity into trance-like states of focus. Actually, it's interesting to note that song and dance commonly feature in mating rituals, perhaps to showcase an ability to maintain rhythm during intercourse.[cxxv]

Millions of us have experienced moments of what the social scientist Jenny Wade refers to as "transcendent sex." This is the kind of sex that, through a neurochemical cocktail of dopamine, oxytocin, and endorphins, can trigger an almost religious state of selflessness and unity, "identical to those attained by spiritual adepts of all traditions."[cxxvi]

It's therefore unfortunate, and also very telling, that sex has been so rigidly controlled or suppressed throughout history, not only by religion. Wilhelm Reich's psychoanalytic emphasis on the importance of orgasm for overall well-being was heavily stigmatized during his lifetime – even by Freud, whose work it apparently influenced. Likewise, the pioneering sexologist Alfred Kinsey was derided and obstructed in his efforts to shed light on the vast range of human sexuality.

Nicole Daedone, founder of OneTaste, is in many ways the successor to Kinsey and Reich – albeit with a far more receptive audience. In true Silicon Valley style, she and her organization have formalized the female orgasm as a Ray Kurzweil-endorsed "technology" for attaining flow states. Known as Orgasmic Meditation (OM), it involves stroking the upper left quadrant of a woman's clitoris to induce a state of neurochemical arousal.

Speaking to a TEDx audience in San Francisco,[cxxvii] Daedone predicted a future in which OM would become almost banal, appearing alongside yoga and meditation as a valid means to induce flow states. As OneTaste's head of marketing Van Vleck put it, "it's like eating breakfast... Instead of a latte, women will have an OM. Because that's what regulates your body."[cxxviii]

Like microdosing, OM is subject to best practice protocols for optimal, or at least reliable, results. Sessions should last exactly 15 minutes, for instance, and involve no romantic gestures whatsoever. "Strokers" should also remain fully clothed, while "strokees" are only required to undress below the waist.[cxxix] The rationale is to create an ideal (in fact non-negotiable) "container" of trust, safety, and efficient reliability – all the more important with OM, or indeed any sexual practice, since orgasm means totally losing control.

Perhaps nowhere is this clearer than in the context of BDSM and the sexual expressions of dominance and submission or sadism and masochism. Until as recently as 2010, shortly before the publication of *Fifty Shades of Grey*, the American Psychiatric Association saw BDSM as pathological. Yet, as a 2017 study demonstrated, it's also an extremely reliable route into flow states. Following roughly one-hour sessions, practitioners had lower levels of cortisol and higher levels of testosterone, both key ingredients of flow.[cxxx] And since BDSM doesn't necessarily involve any rhythmic sexual intercourse, it arguably represents a different modality altogether – channeling focus into the "here and now" through intense stimulation and pointed concentration, as well as, more literally, restricted movement.

Even controlling for trust, risk is no doubt still a factor here. And this is certainly true of extreme sports as well. Big wave surfers, rope-free rock climbers, waterfall kayakers, freedivers, and other athletes commonly report an ecstatic sense of timelessness, transcendence, and merging with nature. BASE jumpers, for instance, can enter a "slow motion" state, even while falling at terminal velocity, allowing them to view their surroundings in intricate detail.

Ultra-endurance athlete Christopher Bergland describes his own pursuit of flow as being as much of a curse as a blessing. Although it continually drove him on to greater and greater accomplishments – including a non-stop 135-mile run through Death Valley and a record-breaking 153.76-mile run in just 24 hours – not one of them was ultimately enough. "Interestingly," he wrote in *Psychology Today*, "this feeling of total connectedness reminded me of taking psilocybin in high school and was like a drug in and of itself. Needless to say, I became fanatically hooked."[cxxxi]

This endless pursuit of flow can, at times, be dangerous. In *Stealing Fire*, Kotler and Wheal give examples of freedivers who died from diving too deep. They also relate the story of extreme skier Kristen Ulmer, who courted death around the world, including on the notorious north face of Aiguille du Midi in Chamonix, France. Like many extreme sports athletes, she was hopelessly hooked on flow, unable to stop pursuing ever greater risks despite knowing they'd eventually kill her. Unlike many others, however, she discovered alternative means for achieving the same effect – specifically, through interactive art, group flow, and meditation, avoiding pre-mature death in the process.

Extreme sports are obviously risky, but even meditation can be destabilizing in unexpected ways. As Vince Horn explained on The Third Wave Podcast,[cxxxii] the assumption that meditation is always safe and positive is groundless. It's crucial to have support, to be aware of what can happen, and to prepare for when it does.

In fact, whether or not a flow state modality can be life-threatening is beside the point. The bliss that it helps to attain should be looked upon as a means to an end, not the end in itself – at least not if we want to bring something out of it, to effect meaningful change in our lives.

This is part of the reason why Fadiman's microdosing protocol includes a third day as a kind of return to baseline, and why Kotler and Wheal advise strict control over how often we use any ecstatic technology.

Practical Considerations for Seeking Flow through Microdosing

If you try microdosing with the specific intent of invoking increased creativity and flow states, there are certain tactics and considerations to keep in mind to increase your odds of success.

Right from the start, your choice of substance could play a role. While many people find they have nearly identical experiences microdosing whether they use psilocybin or LSD, there have been a number of subjective reports that suggest psilocybin leads to more feeling-oriented and self-reflective episodes. LSD, on the other hand, tends to lead to more extroversion, creativity, and focus, and can be better for increasing productivity. If flow states are your goal, in other words, you might have better luck with LSD.

From there, consider the dose. Taking any amount of psychedelic will increase your ability to engage in potentially productive "divergent thinking" that literally diverges from accepted thought constructs. Divergent thinking is typically described as free flowing, spontaneous, and non-linear, as opposed to logic-based "convergent thinking." As a rule of thumb, the higher the dose, the more divergent your thinking tends to be, but the more difficult it usually is to choose what you're thinking about.

Taken to the extreme, a 400-microgram dose of LSD can produce extremely creative, divergent ways of experiencing the world, but would result in a limited ability to determine the object of your attention and productively assimilate your observations and thoughts into a practical plan of action. With that in mind, some individuals specifically seeking to increase their creative output choose to "minidose."

In this context, we'll refer to a minidose as a dose strong enough that it is no longer truly sub-perceptual (all true microdoses are sub-perceptual) but still less than a museum dose. Minidosing can be tremendously impactful for ideation and improving abstract reasoning while still leaving you with enough control to not only fully function in normal circumstances but also to assimilate your divergent thinking into a plan of action.

Finally, it pays to be cautious. As I mentioned in Chapter 4, when you're in a flow state, your impulse control is down regulated; you're more likely to make impulsive decisions.

The best way to mitigate this effect is to maintain conscious self-awareness when you microdose and set rules for making decisions. For example, you could make a rule that you will not make any major decisions while microdosing. Instead, wait 24 hours. "This sounds like a great idea. Give me a night to sleep on it and we can make a decision tomorrow."

It's also a good idea to practice microdosing outside of the context in which you make important decisions. Take time over the weekend or away from work to experience the effects of microdosing on your body and mind. It will help you develop the self-awareness necessary to sidestep these potential pitfalls so you can facilitate a more beneficial experience for yourself.

---

cvii

Mihaly Csikszentmihalyi, *Flow: The Psychology of Optimal Experience* (New York: Harper Perennial Modern Classics , 2008)

cviii

James Fadiman, *The Psychedelic Explorer's Guide: Safe, Therapeutic, and Sacred Journeys* (Rochester, VT: Park Street Press, 2011)

cix

Baynard Woods, "Can very small doses of LSD make you a better worker? I decided to try it.," *Vox*, March 2, 2016, http://www.vox.com/2016/3/2/11115974/lsd-internet-addiction

cx

Katie Herzog, That One Time I Tried to Microdose on LSD, But Accidentally Took Too Much...," *the Stranger*, March 8, 2017, http://www.thestranger.com/features/2017/03/08/25008382/adventures-in-microdosing

cxi

Willis W. Harman and James Fadiman, "Psychedelic Agents in Creative Problem-Solving: A Pilot Study," *Psychedelic Reports* 19 (1966): 211-27, http://www.druglibrary.org/schaffer/lsd/harman.htm

cxii

P.G. Stafford and B.H. Golightly, *LSD — The Problem-Solving Psychedelic* (Award Books, 1967)

cxiii

Benny Shanon, "Ayahuasca and Creativity," *MAPS* volume X, number 3 (2000): 18-19, http://www.maps.org/news-letters/v10n3/10318sha.html

cxiv

Anna Ermakova and Rosalind Stone, "Ayahuasca and Creativity: the Amazonian Plant Brew Improves Divergent Thinking," *Beckley Foundation*, July 29, 2016, http://beckleyfoundation.org/2016/07/29/ayahuasca-and-creativity/

cxv

Neiloufar Family, David Vinson, Gabriella Vigliocco, Mendel Kaelen, Mark Bolstridge, David J. Nutt & Robin L. Carhart-Harris, "Semantic activation in LSD: evidence from picture naming,"

Language, Cognition and Neuroscience Vol. 31 , Iss. 10 (2016): 1320-1327,
http://www.tandfonline.com/doi/abs/10.1080/23273798.2016.1217030
[cxvi]

"LSD and associative thinking," *The Psychedelic Scientist*, October 1, 2016,
https://thepsychedelicscientist.com/2016/10/01/lsd-and-associative-thinking/
[cxvii]

Ian Sample, "LSD's impact on the brain revealed in groundbreaking images," *the Guardian*, April
11, 2016 https://www.theguardian.com/science/2016/apr/11/lsd-impact-brain-revealed-
groundbreaking-images
[cxviii]

Steven Kotler and Jamie Wheal, *Stealing Fire: How Silicon Valley, the Navy SEALs, and Maverick
Scientists Are Revolutionizing the Way We Live and Work* (New York: HarperCollins, 2017)
[cxix]

Shelly Fan, "Floating Away: The Science of Sensory Deprivation Therapy," *Discover*, April 4,
2014, http://blogs.discovermagazine.com/crux/2014/04/04/floating-away-the-science-of-sensory-
deprivation-therapy/
[cxx]

Jamie Wheal, "Jamie Wheal talks about the flow state," uploaded February 15, 2017, podcast,
http://unbeatablemind.com/jamie-wheal/
[cxxi]

Amy Cuddy, "Your body language may shape who you are," filmed June 2012 at TEDGlobal
2012, video, https://www.ted.com/talks/amy_cuddy_your_body_language_shapes_who_you_are
[cxxii]

Esther Eckhart, "The 'flow state' and how to get there," *EkhartYoga*, July 29, 2016,
https://www.ekhartyoga.com/articles/the-flow-state-and-how-to-get-there
[cxxiii]

Steven Kotler and Jamie Wheal, *Stealing Fire: How Silicon Valley, the Navy SEALs, and Maverick
Scientists Are Revolutionizing the Way We Live and Work* (New York: HarperCollins, 2017)
[cxxiv]

"Meditation vs Microdosing," *Reddit*, accessed October 5, 2017,
https://www.reddit.com/r/microdosing/comments/68z5ji/meditation_vs_microdosing/

cxxv

Northwestern University, "Getting into the flow: Sexual pleasure is a kind of trance," *EurekAlert!*, October 31, 2016, https://www.eurekalert.org/pub_releases/2016-10/nu-git103116.php

cxxvi

Jenny Wade, *Transcendent Sex: When Lovemaking Opens the Veil* (New York: Pocket Books, 2004).

cxxvii

TEDx Talks, "TEDxSF - Nicole Daedone - Orgasm: The Cure for Hunger in the Western Woman," *YouTube*, June 11, 2011, https://www.youtube.com/watch?v=s9QVq0EM6g4&vl=en

cxxviii

Nitasha Tiku, "My Life With the Thrill-Clit Cult," *Gawker*, October 16, 2013, http://gawker.com/my-life-with-the-thrill-clit-cult-1445204953

cxxix

OneTaste Inc., *The Container & Form of Orgasmic Meditation* (Revision 1.2.1, 2016), https://onetaste.us/container

cxxx

J. K. Ambler et al., "Consensual BDSM facilitates role-specific altered states of consciousness: A preliminary study," *Psychology of Consciousness: Theory, Research, and Practice*, 4, no. 1: 75-91, http://psycnet.apa.org/doi/10.1037/cns0000097

cxxxi

Christopher Bergland, "Superfluidity and the Transcendent Ecstasy of Extreme Sports," *Psychology Today*, May 10, 2017, https://www.psychologytoday.com/blog/the-athletes-way/201705/superfluidity-and-the-transcendent-ecstasy-extreme-sports

cxxxii

The Third Wave, "Psychedelics for Meditation with Vincent Horn," podcast, https://thethirdwave.co/vince-horn/

Chapter 11: Microdosing for Twenty-First Century Leadership Development

My own leadership path and development is closely tied to microdosing – both the modality itself and the meteoric growth of interest in the topic.

Prior to starting The Third Wave, I had little leadership experience. Most of my decision making, from a business perspective, only impacted myself and a handful of English teaching clients. I did not have a team, and I was not speaking publicly about an incendiary topic like psychedelics.

But I yearned for greater responsibility and influence, so I built The Third Wave into an authority platform about both microdosing and, generally, the responsible use of psychedelics. As a relatively privileged white male from the United States, I knew it would be easier for me to speak out about these substances in a personal, story-telling format that would connect with the mainstream audience I wanted to target. Further, I embodied the "typical" leadership qualities: charismatic, confident, well-spoken, with a propensity to conceptualize new ideas that resonated with other people on a purpose-driven level.

Because this perfect storm of my life came together, I took it upon myself to begin The Third Wave, and self-organize a microdosing speaking tour across the States and Europe. During the year of 2017, I found out what it meant to become a leader, in both a positive and negative sense.

Positives:

- Building a vision that aligns with people on a purpose driven level to contribute to a cause and mission that is bigger than themselves but that they are still personally invested in.

- Speaking the truth about an uncomfortable topic by using my position of privilege to speak for those who can't.
- Cultivating and developing skills that directly relate to social intelligence and public speaking.
- Empowering team members to take responsibility for their role within an organization, and using their own purpose and passion in making a significant contribution. It isn't about the money – they will gladly work more hours without worrying about compensation.

Negatives:

- Learning how to deal with direct, personal criticism about a topic of sensitivity (must not personalize criticism, even if harsh).
- Not prioritizing self-care, which leads to burnout and ineffectiveness over the long-term.

Overall, the lessons I learned about leadership via microdosing in 2017 played a foundational role in my own personal development and the theoretical framework we will lay out in the rest of this chapter.

As the world evolves and we continue to develop new technology at a breathtaking pace, the demands of leadership in the 21st century are becoming starkly different than they were in the past. Change is happening faster than ever, and leaders need to be able to adapt quickly to new situations and bring an entrepreneurial spirit to their endeavors. Microdosing can help accelerate the developmental process for the next generation of leaders by unlocking qualities such as creativity, adaptability, and honest self-reflection that will push them toward the pinnacle of their professions.

Change is the defining characteristic of business in the internet age, while the ability to adapt to change and solve problems is one of the most important effects of microdosing. These changes provide both exciting new opportunities as well as great risks. Legacy business plans can crumble in an instant while new models spring up seemingly overnight to take their place.

People are connected like never before through mobile and internet technology, and even a growing number of our objects and devices are hooked into the larger web, communicating with one another and collecting and analyzing data that we might not even realize exists.

New technologies, new leadership tools, new culture

Given the momentous possibilities afforded by technology, great leaders are charged with coming up with creative solutions to unexpected issues and problems, turning potential setbacks to their advantage. If your business model isn't disrupting an industry, you can bet that someone is going to come along soon to disrupt you. Rest on your laurels without striving to be several steps ahead of your competitors, and you are lost. Arriving at the forefront of your field requires mastering new technology and being open to novel ways of accomplishing tasks, taking both short and long term needs into account – or seeing with a microscope and a telescope, as a McKinsey leadership forum put it.[cxxxiii]

Companies today operate in a dynamic environment where changes happen quickly and unexpectedly, turning over entire segments of a market in an instant. Look at the effect Uber and Lyft on the taxicab industry. For decades, the taxi cab model was essentially unchallenged for spontaneous, private transport around a city if you didn't have access to your personal car. Municipalities charged high fees to license taxis and imposed heavy regulations, while lack of competition allowed the services to stagnate. Then ride-hailing companies used the power of mobile technology to connect passengers and drivers using an app on their cell phones. It was fast, convenient, and easy. The new models took over a huge share of the market nearly overnight, with cities powerless to stop them even when they tried to protect traditional taxi cabs. That's the kind of sea change that entrepreneurial leadership can create.

Sometimes, changes are imposed from the outside. Leadership is most important in moments of crisis or momentous disturbance, when people look to an individual who can guide them through the shifting landscapes and provide clear and insightful decision-making. Upheaval can be impossible to predict, whether through a market-shifting event or a natural disaster. Shifting alliances, war, migration, an ever-growing human population, and environmental instability all add to the volatile era in which we live. This requires leaders with vision to help create a better future.

Even on a more day-to-day level, the nature of work has changed dramatically, rewarding those who are able to be flexible, another benefit that microdosing provides. For many, particularly those in leadership positions, work is no longer a nine-to-five operation. Rather, people with decision-making capabilities often need to be accessible at any moment to respond to challenges or emergencies that arise. On the other side of the coin, clever entrepreneurs are setting up businesses that can operate for days or months at a time with little maintenance, creating a revenue stream while freeing them to pursue other activities.

My personal experience reflects this last sentiment. I built my online English teaching business with this exact goal in mind. Like most young entrepreneurs who read Tim Ferriss's *The 4-Hour Work Week*, I envisioned a future of sitting on remote beaches in Thailand, sipping a coconut and soaking in the beautiful rays. While it took slightly longer than expected, my preference for optionality over accumulation created enough freedom where, had I so chosen, such a situation would have been possible. But instead of chasing women and sipping cocktails, I spent the extra time building The Third Wave as a premier psychedelic resource.

Some jobs require near constant travel to check in on far-flung locations or attend events and speaking engagements around the world. Fortunately, technology and connectivity make it easy to stay in touch and monitor operations no matter where in the world you are. Humanity has created a novel situation where we can be tied to work in some capacity 24 hours a day, yet afforded the freedom to travel and mold our work environment to best fit our needs and comfort.

What's your comfort level? Even if you cut your teeth in a traditional workforce, and prefer the trappings of a nine-to-five office, you need to be flexible. Not only can a business sink or swim by decisions made (or not) over a night or weekend, but many young workers expect more flexibility in their working conditions, and more meaning to their work. If you fail to meet those needs, you might find your best employees leaving for someone who does.

Furthermore, leadership is adapting to be less hierarchical, dominant, and aggressive, and more about curating and cultivating space to allow the best people to step in and contribute. Here the Uber example is also instructive in a more negative way. Following the company's quick ascension to the top of the ride-sharing market, the senior leadership was rapidly enveloped in scandal and dissatisfaction. The company has taken serious flack for a range of issues from a lack of respect to rider privacy to a patriarchal, misogynistic culture that stretched from the executive offices down to reports of harassment alleged against individual drivers.[cxxxiv] Co-founder Travis Kalanick was ultimately forced out as CEO following unrelenting reports of wrongdoing. The saga serves to demonstrate how the culture of top-down, coercion-based leadership is falling out of style. Great leadership is about more than just disrupting an industry – it's about creating a positive culture where employees are empowered to be their best selves.

An important aspect of this alternative requires chipping away at the ego, which microdosing helps to accomplish. Leaders need to be able to set their defense of their self-image aside to take honest feedback from team members and accept criticism as an opportunity to improve. They need to be secure in themselves to admit when they are wrong but not lose confidence in their vision.

What's more, we can collect feedback from a far wider net than we could just a few years ago. Social media provides opportunity for instant access to communication to millions of people, but the same time you must be cautious because a misstatement can turn to scandal in a moment. The feedback you receive can be useful, harsh, voluminous, and you have to be prepared to acknowledge all of it. Leaders must be able to take input from a wide diversity of sources, consider it openly, and move forward with sound decisions.

Thinking and feeling

Leaders also need to know when to follow their gut and when to take a more analytic approach to problems. In my own work, I refer to this as the balance between "thinking" and "feeling." While analytical thinking is necessary in a world of logic and science, intuition also has its role, particularly in a 21st century world that values relationships.

In my process of building The Third Wave, I continue to find the best ways of balancing these two important ways of being. I have, on several occasions, hired other team members to contribute in a way that is in line with their skill sets. When determining this fit, I had to create clear expectations of the tasks each individual would carry out.

At the same time, my feeling and intuition of who the person was, and the values that dictated their work, hold even greater importance in the long run. Over the course of growing The Third Wave, I hired a few people that within a few weeks I knew were not right for the job. It wasn't a conclusion I came to by analysis, as they had all the necessary skill sets on paper. Instead, it was a gut feeling of "our values and principles aren't in alignment." Within this process, I had to reverse my original commitment, admit my wrongdoing in onboarding the specific individual, and adjust my approach to ensure all hired team members were onboard with the larger vision (and in it for the "right" reasons).

You may find you need to question your deepest assumptions and most strongly held values if they are holding you back. The most effective leaders know how to exercise authority, delegate tasks and manage people – and adjust when their tactics aren't working for a particular personality. This often requires a significant degree of self-honesty.

Author Tony Schwartz in the *Harvard Business Review* suggests the key to 21st century leadership is to "become more wholly human – to actively develop a wider range of capabilities and to more deeply understand themselves."[cxxxv] Many of the qualities we associate with good leadership, he writes, such as confidence, pragmatism, and decisiveness, can actually hold us back if we over-rely on them and allow them to become arrogance, unimaginativeness, and dogmatism. Instead, we need to be able to step past our old bindings and consider exercising qualities that are the opposite of what we have become accustomed to: think humility, imaginativeness, and open-mindedness. That doesn't mean you should forget the old qualities you used to become a leader in the first place, you just need to find the self-awareness to know when to balance them with what appear to be their opposites.

"The goal is not to find a perfect balance," Schwartz wrote, "but to build a complementary set of strengths, so that we can move gracefully along a spectrum of leadership qualities. Embracing our own complexity makes us more wholly human and gives us additional resources to manage ourselves and others in an increasingly complex world."

4 quadrants of management

One function of the world's increasing complexity is the way work is changing. In his book *The End of Jobs: Money, Meaning and Freedom Without the 9-to-5,*[cxxxvi] author Taylor Pearson explains the Cynefin framework, a tool developed by Dave Snowden to divide up work and management in a way that reflects that change. The framework chops management into four quadrants:

- Simple: when the cause and effect of an issue is clear
- Complicated: when a solution requires more analysis
- Complex: when the right response can't be figured out through past experience or education
- Chaotic: when the relationship between cause and effect is dissolved and you need to come up with completely new ways to move forward

The tool includes a series of steps toward reaching an outcome. The steps are:

- Best practice
- Good practice
- Emergent practice
- Novel practice

In today's world, simple and even complicated issues are falling by the wayside, subject to mechanization or otherwise becoming obsolete. True leaders are immersing themselves in the worlds of complex and chaotic problems, developing totally novel approaches to problem solving.

As a consequence, one of the tried and true pillars of good leadership in the past, implementing and following best practices to reach a desired outcome, is less important than ever. Best practices are a fine way to resolve simple problems, but groundbreaking leaders today are functioning in a world far beyond simple problems. While people whose business concepts are grounded in the 20th century are concerning themselves with best practices, their entire industries are changing underneath them. The leaders who will succeed tomorrow are taking an entrepreneurial approach to tackling complex and chaotic issues, driving change in their field instead of struggling to catch up or risking being left behind altogether.

Pearson writes of Eli Goldratt, former head of Creative Output, a software company that focused on production optimization. Goldratt's work sought to increase work output by identifying and addressing bottlenecks in a production process, therefore multiplying the effects of his efforts by allowing other more efficient parts of the process to not get slowed down by one, poorly performing system. "There are three basic questions to ask when applying Goldratt's framework," Pearson writes. "What's the system? What's the current limit? What's the obvious way to improve the limit?"

The Third Wave is an excellent example of this way of thinking. Building the groundwork for a business model around illegal substances appears naive, if not downright stupid. Had I simply followed best practices in deciding which project to start after my online teaching business, I would have chosen something safe and secure, that already has a clear path to profitability (one super cool idea I had with a close friend was to give interactive tours of museums; museums are, and will always be, legal!).

Instead, by choosing to begin The Third Wave, I chose to tackle one of the more complex issues of our time: the prohibition of certain illicit substances that have clear medical and psychospiritual benefit for the end user. Before taking this leap, I analyzed a number of other factors, including the growth in psychedelic research, the legalization of cannabis, and the use of microdosing by the tech world. At that point, I decided to go ahead with the project.

Pearson makes an excellent point about tackling just that sort of complexity. He argues that as a society, we have run up against a limit for overall growth and production by focusing on solving simple problems while receiving diminishing returns. That leaves us vulnerable to stagnation and job loss, creating a drag on progress and a drain on resources. Instead, if we shift our attentions to tackling complex and chaotic problems, we can surpass our current limits and move into a new economic era.

In fact, according to Pearson, although most people consider it risky to try new ways of doing things like I did with The Third Wave, entrepreneurship is actually safer than it's ever been. While you might be reluctant to take the risk of starting your own venture, the potential rewards can far outweigh the drawbacks. Because of a cognitive tendency called loss aversion, we are more swayed by the potential of losing something than the benefits of what we could gain. But for most of us, failure in a modern business setting doesn't mean you are relegated to a life of poverty and humiliation. Usually, it's a temporary setback, especially to people with a strong drive to succeed. If you have a great idea that can make a real difference in the world today, imagine the vast rewards you could reap and don't get dissuaded by the consequences of failure unless they are truly threatening to your life or well-being.

Furthermore, sometimes the paths that look sane, sensible, or risk-free can leave you vulnerable to outside forces that could throw all your plans into disarray anyway. If you aren't constantly adapting to stay ahead of looming changes in today's world, you are in fact accumulating silent risk that could build up and harm you when you can least afford it. Pearson uses the example of an accountant who sticks with a steady job, only to be blindsided by a layoff when the company finds a cheaper way to perform the same function. By contrast, an accountant who takes what appears to be a riskier path of starting his own company has greater control of his destiny, is building new skills and relationships and has a greater capacity to carve out his own role in society. The more entrepreneurial among us don't build up silent risk because they are forced to constantly adjust their product or services to meet the current and future needs of the market.

In the modern world, the three motivations shown by research to be most important to humans are money, freedom, and meaning, Pearson writes. When many people think about the profession they intend to follow, they focus on money first, and maybe meaning if they are lucky. However, given the technological tools at our hands today, it's easier than ever for smart leaders and entrepreneurs to pursue all three goals at once. This can even have an amplifying effect, because if you feel like your work is a meaningful choice, not a rote obligation, you are likely to do a better job, thereby increasing the amount of money you earn in the end. "Freedom and meaning aren't something to be put off until after you're rich—they help you get rich," Pearson writes.

"Great work—the kind of work that will create wealth in our lives and the lives of others is not the product of obligation—is the product of freedom," the author continues. "Freedom gives us a longer lever, a better leverage point. By seeking more freedom and building it into our lives, we not only improve our ability to create more material wealth and make more money personally, but we also create more of it in the world at large."

Ultimately, these ideas all come back to Hungarian psychologist Mihaly Csikszentmihalyi's concept of flow. When people become consumed with meeting a goal or overcoming a challenge, immersed in finding new and better ways of completing a task, they feel most happy and fulfilled, and at the same time create even more valuable work.

"As a society, we're paying people more money to do things which create less wealth," writes Pearson. "Yet we're at a point where we can create more wealth and make more money for ourselves and others by pursuing work which forces us to grow in a way we personally find meaningful."

Tribal leadership: a new renaissance

In the book *Tribal Leadership*, authors Dave Logan, John King, and Halee Fischer-Wright lay out another framework to explain how great leadership can elevate companies and individuals to new levels of excellence by inspiring actions aimed toward the common good.[cxxxvii] While Tribal Leadership does not touch on microdosing, I've found that many of the qualities and strategies the authors invoke as important components to unlocking the highest levels of success are attributes that microdosing can help to unleash – such as big-picture vision, empathy, and the ability to make decisions that aren't wrapped up within the ego.

This outlook is based on the premise that while the world may not be broken, it can be far better than it is today. While the civilizations of ancient Greece and Rome, and later Europe during the Renaissance created the foundations of our modern world, those advances really only targeted society's elite, excluding most others.

Today, the authors envision a new renaissance, one that's based on merit alone and not restricted to any particular location or identity group. Instead, it relies on raising the effectiveness of business cultures, which by and large are bastions of mediocrity, to unleash the potential of the individuals within them.

The authors lay out a model of different cultural stages that organizations find themselves in and explore how to accelerate the transition into higher levels of functioning, which will in turn attract more people who want to make a real contribution. Culture, in this context, covers both the words that people use to describe themselves, one another, and their work, as well as the structure of relationships and how people are connected to one another.

We often think of humanity as grouped into tribes, or groups of 150 or fewer people.[cxxxviii] Those within a particular tribe tend to exhibit certain behaviors, talking and acting in a particular manner. *Tribal Leadership* focuses on culture because the culture of a tribe is stronger than the effect that any one individual can exert. For example, in the context of a business's various departments or groups, we're likely to gain more value from introducing a cultural change across the group than we would from changing a single person's work. And just as a positive culture can elevate an entire business, an inept or negative one can hold everyone back, even those individuals who would otherwise be high achievers.

"Tribal culture exists in stages, going from undermining to egocentric to history making," the authors write. "Some tribes demand excellence for everyone, and are constantly evolving. Others are content to do the minimum to get by. What makes the difference in performance? Tribal Leaders." If tribal leaders are successfully able to upgrade the culture of their organization, the members (or employees) should respond with their best work. And when everyone is on board and engaged with the work, the tribe or company can produce results that far exceed what any individual, including the leader, could produce alone.

The authors break down tribal culture into five stages:

Stage one
This is a group operating at survival level – comprised of people who are despairingly hostile and have no hope of achieving a better life. In the professional world, they estimate that only 2 percent of tribes fall into stage one.

Stage two
The second stage is larger, making up 25 percent of the employed population, according to the authors. While not as desperate as stage one, it is still defined

by negativity – but negativity confined to individual circumstances, not the hopelessness of the world at large. "People in this cultural stage are passively antagonistic; they cross their arms in judgment yet never really get interested enough to spark any passion," they write. "Their laughter is quietly sarcastic and resigned. The Stage Two talk is that they've seen it all before and watched it all fail."

Notably, even people who have the drive and desire to reach a higher level individually can get bogged down and fail to thrive if all their peers are in a stage two group. Instead, everyone would have a better chance to advance if the entire tribe could be pulled into stage three by effective leadership.

Stage three

Here is where most professional cultures in the U.S. are located and is identifiable by excellence – but excellence of the individual, not of the group.

"Within the Stage Three culture, knowledge is power, so people hoard it, from client contacts to gossip about the Company," the authors state. "People at Stage Three have to win, and for them winning is personal. They'll out-work and outthink their competitors on an individual basis." Many companies encourage stage three behavior by measuring the success of the individual and creating situations where high performers are given a chance to shine, and workers are pitted against one another for rewards like resources and promotions.

You can recognize stage three cultures by the predominance of first-person identifiers like "I" and "my," and a paucity of collaboration, culture-wide innovation, or awareness of shared values.

Stage four

By contrast, Stage four is characterized by collective core values and group members working together toward a shared goal. About 22 percent of tribes fall into the stage four classification, and enormous opportunity exists for effective leaders to usher groups from stage three to stage four and release new waves of creativity and success.

The benefits of fostering a stage four culture are myriad, including a reduction in fear, stress, and friction as collaboration increases and competition is left aside. Morale and general health indicators improve. "The entire tribe shifts from resisting leadership to seeking it out," according to the book. "Setting and implementing a successful competitive strategy becomes stunningly easy as people's aspirations, knowledge of the market, and creativity are unlocked and shared. Most exciting for us is that people report feeling more alive and having more fun."

Start by developing yourself

The key question, then, is how leaders can transition a group from stage three to stage four – and how microdosing can play a role in that process. To earn the respect, trust, and buy-in of your peers, you need to first do work on yourself. Start by making sure you understand the language and customs of people who are functioning at different stages, so you can meet them at their level and present ideas and concepts in a way that makes sense. At the same time, you need to advance yourself into stage four, and try to bring a core group of people with you to create a center of gravity that exerts a positive influence on the rest of the tribe.

People have frequently found themselves shaken out of stage three into a more collaborative stage four attitude by major life changes, such as turning forty and transitioning into middle age, or by losing a loved one. These events can inspire people to want to give back more to the world, as opposed to focusing only on personal achievement. Notably, a paradigm-shifting experience with moderate doses of psychedelics can have the same result.

When you're ready to move forward in your leadership journey, ask yourself what your ultimate goal is, what you want to accomplish most of all. "As the person sees into her blind spots she realizes that the ego hit of accomplishment isn't the same as success itself," writes Logan, King, and Fischer-Wright . "Her attention shifts to what's really important to her, and almost always, the goal is tribal."

From there, you can start to influence the others around you. "Instead of speaking for herself and assuming that others will see the logic in her point of view, she begins to listen, to learn about the tribe, and to speak for it," the authors continue. "As all this happens, a subtle but rapid change begins: she accrues respect, loyalty, followers, and an expectation of great things."

This change occurs when you purposefully shift language away from saying "me" and "I" toward words that encompass the goals of the entire group. Language is an important indicator of culture and an intentional shift can often lead to a more collaborate mindset. When you start talking more about a common good, it's not that you lose your ego, or your drive to succeed, it's that you learn to direct those things toward the group overall instead of toward individual accolades. You also gain the ability to observe your ego so you aren't controlled by it, helping you to see and judge yourself objectively so you can make decisions that lead to the best outcome, not ones that just make you look or feel accomplished.

When you are confident that you are operating in a stage four space yourself, you are ready to flex your leadership and bring your tribe along with you. Remember, the core values of the group should be the primary driving force of the organization. Know what values are respected in the group and use language and tactics that reflect them.

To start elevating your colleagues, ask them an escalating series of questions to identify their core values. For example, question someone about what they're proud of, then ask why, and continue to ask why for each response they give you until they stop being able to clearly articulate the reason something is important – an indicator that you have reached a core value, because it's so ingrained that it can defy expression.

From the outside, you may be able to better articulate the value than the person who holds it. Once you discover the values of all the people in your tribe, and can express them as a common vision, your leadership will really start to take off.

Continue to grow your group into stage four by showing the people around you that networks are more important to building power than knowledge, and impress on them that a team working in unison can achieve far more than a single person. Build your team's network by reaching out to people you know who share your values. Create mutually beneficial relationships. Leverage the competitive spirit inherent in stage three but direct it toward other groups or companies, not other individuals.

Tribal Leadership also recommends streamlining an approach to building a strategy, based on three conversations:

- What we want (outcomes)
- What we have (assets)
- What we will do (behaviors)

"The last epiphany is seeing that the only real goal is the betterment of the tribe," the authors write. "Ironically, as people act to build the tribe they achieve everything they sought but couldn't achieve at Stage Three: esteem, respect, loyalty, legacy, and enduring success."

Unfortunately, our professional world is defined by stage three behaviors, with people competing to acquire more and more for themselves, regardless of consequences. Witness banks, pharmaceutical companies, the extraction industry, and others – lying, cheating, doing whatever it takes to bring in profits no matter how harmful to individuals or to the world. Stage three behavior is defined in part by an inability to reflect on itself.

The more companies that start operating at a self-aware, value-driven stage four level, the better off *everyone* will be as we begin to leave behind antisocial behaviors and strive toward outcomes that transcend the egos of the individuals involved.

Stage five
This represents only two percent of professional tribes in the U.S. "Their language revolves around infinite potential and how the group is going to

make history—not to beat a competitor, but because doing so will make a global impact," the authors write. According to the authors: "This group's mood is 'innocent wonderment,' with people in competition with what's possible, not with another tribe." Stage five groups are the visionaries who change the world.

Most leaders who read this book will see an immediate opportunity to elevate their groups from stage three to stage four. But the truly transcendent, those who can harness their collective values into groundbreaking innovation, can create stage five groups and help lead humanity toward a better future.

Make it a better world

All of the requirements to succeed as a ground-breaking entrepreneur in the 21st century – the ability to come up with creative solutions that address complex or chaotic problems, the capacity to self-reflect honestly and incorporate feedback from a variety of sources into your processes, and the power to tap into a flow state to produce your best, most meaningful work – are things that microdosing can help with. Microdosing alone won't make you a great entrepreneur, but it does hold the potential to unlock the qualities that leaders need to develop and carry out their visions in a dynamic and fast-changing world.

The leaders who will be successful are those who can form a coherent vision of the future and piece together more accurate models of where the world is going – and how to make it better. As humans come to recognize that we are sharing a planet with dwindling natural resources, we are starting to realize the futility of a zero-sum competitive business model, with more and more companies moving toward a collaborative, entrepreneurial model of sharing.

Society's true leaders will use their skills not only to create ventures that make themselves more fulfilled, but to come up with ground-breaking new concepts that transform and improve the whole world.

cxxxiii

http://www.mckinsey.com/global-themes/leadership/leading-in-the-21st-century

cxxxiv

https://qz.com/917179/uber-is-racking-up-one-star-reviews-in-the-ios-app-store/

cxxxv

https://hbr.org/2017/07/how-to-become-a-more-well-rounded-leader

cxxxvi

https://www.amazon.com/End-Jobs-Meaning-9-5-ebook/dp/B010L8SYRG/ref=sr_1_1?ie=UTF8&qid=1501075345&sr=8-1&keywords=end+of+jobs

cxxxvii

http://www.triballeadership.net/book

cxxxviii

This is also called the 'Dunbar Number', popularized by British anthropologist Robin Dunbar, who found a correlation between primate brain size and average social group size

Chapter 12: Finished Your Microdosing Protocol? What's Next?

When I stopped my first microdosing protocol in January 2016, I did so out of necessity.

Seven months of microdosing LSD two times per week had gone off without a hitch: my creative projects flourished, I had more confidence and charisma in social situations, and I excelled in my ability to articulate thoughts and ideas in a clear, meaningful manner.

Yet, I had plans to leave Thailand and travel to Taiwan, and chose to minimize my own personal risk by not carrying any sort of illicit substance with me.

At the time, I was ambivalent stopping my protocol. On the one hand, I felt a deep sense of contentment for the transformation in my own life, and had yet to experience any sort of negative consequences. On the other hand, I did not want to become psychologically dependent on an external substance for engendering transformation. Further, I did not know enough about the risks of consistently taking low amounts of LSD over an extended period of time.

You may find yourself at a similar crossroads after finishing your first microdosing protocol.

One way to find a middle ground is to microdose every so often during the intervening period between protocols.[cxxxix] You may choose to do this as a practical boost in your working life, or in conjunction with some of the activities discussed in the last chapter.

Above all, though, you should use this time to get back to baseline and enquire into what's changed since you started. Dig back through your old notes and journals and take a critical look at how you've developed. Ask yourself:

- Have I achieved the goals I set out to (or have my priorities shifted)?
- Am I approaching my work, relationships, health, and other areas of my life any differently?
- Has my self image changed?
- How do I feel about the future?
- What about the past?
- Have I learned anything else?

It may be useful to go over these points with somebody who knows you well, especially when it comes to relationships. This could be a significant other, a close friend, or even a therapist. Ideally, they'll have seen you frequently throughout your microdosing protocol – whether or not they knew you were doing it – and be able to gauge any changes.

The final question – whether you learned anything else (for example about yourself, others, or life in general) – may be the most important. Microdosing can have surprising and very personal outcomes, shining a light on previously hidden parts of your psyche. Ultimately, by taking time away from it, you'll be able to identify clear practical foci for future cycles.

From microdosing to macrodosing and back again

If you haven't previously done so, you could also use this time to see what else psychedelics have to offer. After all, long before the current explosion of interest in microdosing, psychedelics were transforming lives in profound ways through isolated, sometimes one-off mystical experiences. It's easy to lose sight of this while microdosing and come to view psychedelics in purely functional, everyday terms. And while this no doubt eases their acceptance by the (relative) mainstream, it only gives part of the picture.

When thinking about the intersection between microdosing and "macrodosing," or taking a full trip, we can talk in broad terms about the biochemical on the one hand and the psychospiritual on the other. To put it another way, whereas microdosing is integrated into daily life as a kind of biochemical aid, macrodosing forces a more rigorous and overwhelming look at what daily life means in the first place. One is sub-perceptual; the other is hyper-perceptual. One is practical, grounded in worldly activities; the other is philosophical, questioning the assumptions behind them.

Clearly, full doses have the potential to meaningfully inform and direct a microdosing practice – complementing the largely results-driven protocols with deep introspective enquiry into the results you really need.

There's reciprocity between these two modalities by which insights from one can feed into the other. On a full dose of psilocybin or LSD, for instance, you might come to realize the extent of dysfunction that you've allowed to creep into relationships – an issue your next cycle of microdosing can then empower you to address with action. Conversely, while microdosing, you might discover things about yourself, such as ingrained resistances, deep-seated alienation, historic trauma, and so forth that you'd like to explore in more detail. In this case, you can set a clear intention to do so before going into a full trip. This is also a way of contextualizing and integrating the whole experience.

At a more practical level, taking a full dose of psychedelics can help to prepare you in case of accidentally taking too much while microdosing. Instead of shock and confusion to the point of panic, you'll at least know what to expect – even if an accidental trip may still be undesirable.

Of course, full doses have lasting benefits of their own, quite apart from microdosing. In addition to the sometimes life-changing insights and realizations gleaned from the trip itself, people commonly report an "afterglow" effect that lasts for days, weeks, or even months afterward – in contrast to the sometimes short-lived or dose-dependent benefits of microdosing. A noticeably brighter mood and higher levels of compassion, empathy, and self-esteem characterize this afterglow state. It can be especially useful for sufferers of depression and/or social anxiety.

Even more so than microdosing, however, full trips demand respect and careful preparation. To avoid a negative experience, it's crucial to optimize your mindset and surroundings beforehand. These are often referred to as the "set and setting." We offer plenty of tips for refining them at The Third Wave website.

They include:

- Allowing at least one day[cxl] either side of your trip to prepare for and integrate the experience – ideally in nature.
- Ensuring your space is clean and uncluttered or, if outside, as calm and pleasant as you can find.
- Choosing music that's going to facilitate your desired state of mind, avoiding harsh, jarring sounds and negative lyrics.
- Finding a responsible sitter, at least for your first time – someone with the time, patience, and personal experience to reassure you if things go bad.

Above all, do your research. Like microdosing, macrodosing isn't for everyone. However, if you've had success with the former and find yourself wanting to forge a stronger relationship with psychedelics, then taking a full dose can be a transformative and rewarding next step – potentially also laying the foundations for your next cycle of microdosing.

When to Microdose Again?

The question remains: when should you restart your microdosing protocol?

After my initial seven-month microdosing protocol, I stopped an intentional microdosing protocol for approximately one year. During the intervening period, I microdosed from time-to-time – usually with friends in the woods or at a particularly impressive museum – but did not follow any sort of regimen.

I chose to begin another microdosing protocol because I was beginning to carry out an extensive public speaking tour. Based on my original experience with microdosing, I knew my ability to articulate concepts and ideas significantly improved while on small amounts of LSD.

When determining whether or not to start another microdosing protocol, intention is the most important aspect.

Do you have a specific reason in mind as to why it would prove beneficial to microdose again? Do you have a boundary of time in which you've set clear benchmarks to measure whether or not microdosing has been effective? Do you have a clear plan to integrate other beneficial habits with your next microdosing protocol so as not to become psychologically reliant on it?

All of these are important considerations when deciding whether or not to begin another microdosing protocol.

---

cxxxix

Again, we simply don't have the data to recommend a definitive duration for this intervening period, or even to say whether it's necessary to begin with. After a normal, i.e. non-micro, dose, LSD clears the system within a day – although certain metabolites can last longer. With microdosing, there may also be a cumulative effect whereby the molecule builds up over time. As a general rule erring on the side of caution, we'd tentatively suggest that a month is more than sufficient.

cxl

At least in the case of LSD and psilocybin. Some other psychedelics may need longer.

Conclusion

Knowledge and awareness of microdosing is quickly becoming ubiquitous. From the offices of Silicon Valley to the pages of popular magazines, the practice is almost impossible to ignore. The prevalence and positive results of microdosing demonstrate its efficacy while breaking down stigma and helping to legitimize psychedelics in the eyes of mainstream society.

While microdosing is a new trend – hip, sexy, and popular with tech entrepreneurs – it is far from a passing fad. In the explosion of interest in microdosing, we are witnessing the birth of a new paradigm in psychedelic use, and this is just the beginning.

As I wrote in the beginning of this book, The Third Wave is named for the new awareness about psychedelics. The first wave was the use of various natural substances such as psilocybin, ayahuasca, ibogaine, and mescaline by indigenous people all over the world – practices that date back thousands of years and often have important spiritual, religious, ceremonial, or health aspects to them. The second wave was the introduction of psychedelics to the western world in the 1960s via figures such as Aldous Huxley and Timothy Leary who popularized the use of LSD.

After a cultural backlash, the U.S. government led the pack in what amounted to worldwide prohibition of many psychedelics, including categorical criminalization, widespread derision, and fear-mongering abetted by the popular media. For decades, psychedelics were widely viewed as dangerous and subversive.

Today, the renewed flood of research into the benefits of psychedelics combined with the popularity of microdosing brings us to the third wave. With diligence and outreach, we can unlock the benefits of psychedelics for a modern society that is desperately in need of them.

Psychedelics can help address an underlying challenge to modern society: the lack of human connection. They remind us to be grateful for our friends, family, and the beauty of life itself. They deepen our empathy and help connect us with nature, spirituality, and the universe as a whole. By reducing our egos, we can concentrate on pure creation without the shackles of feeling judged by others.

One path forward for the legitimization of psychedelics is the wealth of evidence about their efficacy in fighting mental disorders. A lasting, holistic method of combatting harmful problems such as depression, anxiety, PTSD, and addiction is more important than ever in a world filled with trauma and upheaval. Psychedelics give people a way to attack the root of their problems without relying on pharmaceutical companies.

However, while scientific research is one avenue toward legitimizing the consumption of psychedelics in the eyes of the law and society, it might not be enough on its own to break down the barriers between people and these substances. Microdosing, once proven safe and effective and embraced by many of society's leaders, is another method of removing the stigma that psychedelics have faced for decades.

"What can we do to move the psychedelic realities into the general culture?" Jim Fadiman asked his audience during a presentation at the Psychedelic Science 2017 summit in Oakland. "Microdoses don't scare anybody."[cxli]

Microdosing holds the key to the third wave because people are irrational. Facts and research alone aren't enough to sway many of us who have been conditioned to fear and hate psychedelics by decades of propaganda. However, engaging with people on a cultural level, showing examples of people using microdosing to become happier and more successful, provides a means of connection and can open the door to a different mindset. To put it another way, microdosing is an amplifier and accelerator of what is already happening; it does not detach or disconnect us.

The more research and reports that emerge, the more people will feel free to talk openly about these substances, leading to even more public acceptance. For far too long, psychedelics have been taboo, subject to misinformation and propaganda, demonized for political purposes. The prohibition of psychedelics is one of the greatest failures of scientific and political institutions in modern history, a massive setback to the cause of a more just and equitable society.

The stigma is still powerful today, discouraging people from even considering psychedelics as anything other than harmful, destructive drugs. In her book, Ayelet Waldman described a friend's reaction when she revealed that she had been microdosing LSD:

> Her face froze. If she had been wearing pearls, she would have clutched them. She looked horrified, even disgusted, as if I'd told her that I'd taken up murdering baby seals. Her husband's reaction was only slightly less disturbing. He smiled uncomfortably and changed the subject. I immediately agreed, yes, the antipasto was delicious, and, no, I didn't want any more.
>
> Their reaction launched a series of cascading anxieties. Will I be condemned for doing this? Will people reject me as a nutcase, a crank, a deluded acid freak? Will I lose whatever credibility I have in the world? Will parents not let their children come over to our house any more, under the misapprehension that I keep drugs in my home?[cxlii]

The prospect of negative reactions and ostracization could have prevented her from trying the very practice that she credited with saving her marriage.

A more rational legal regime could be on the horizon. Over the past decade, many of the government's claims about cannabis have been stripped away as people have come to realize that the substance poses little harm and can provide significant medical and other benefits. Little by little, both the stigma and the legal restrictions on cannabis have fallen aside and a plethora of new research has been unleashed, providing us with even more understanding of the plant. Psychedelics could be on the same track, although they face larger barriers than marijuana because fewer people have used them. However, microdosing is bringing psychedelics to a whole new population that can go on to advocate for them.

"The information that's increasingly coming out about microdosing makes it more likely that [legalization of LSD] will happen sooner than later," Drug Policy Alliance founder Ethan Nadelmann said during an interview with the Verge.[cxliii] "It's presenting a growing segment of the public with a new perspective on LSD, and it's something that really shatters the images of LSD that people may have in their minds."

"LSD is a totally amazing substance," psychopharmacologist Ralph Metzner said in the same article. "Because it is so potent, and such tiny amounts and tiny differences in tiny amounts make such a huge difference . . . Its sensitivity is off the charts. There's no other drug that comes close to that kind of sensitivity."

Microdosing is an important tool to initiate conversations about psychedelics on a mainstream level. Conversations like these will start the ball rolling toward legitimizing psychedelics and making them available to people who could benefit from them. This wave is already underway, with meetups and groups dedicated to discussing psychedelics and sharing stories and tips popping up in cities all around the globe.

Today it is more crucial than ever to have these types of cultural conversations. Income inequality is soaring, leaving a large and growing share of wealth and power in the hands of a few families and corporations, exposing billions of others to poverty. Authoritarian governments are flexing their muscles around the world, using their power to suppress dissent and harm their weakest and most vulnerable citizens. Basic necessities like healthcare and education are out of reach to a growing number of families. And the climate and environment are on the brink of irrevocable disaster, if not already over the edge, to the extent we have to confront the question of whether the planet will continue to be able to sustain human life in the fast-approaching future.

Psychedelics are not a cure-all for the world's ills; it would be folly to claim that they are. They can, however, help bring enhanced empathy and a greater feeling of connection with nature to more and more people, which can help push the overall attitude and trajectory of human discourse and politics toward a more healthy state.

Just as psychedelics help individuals come to terms with past traumas and see beyond their egos to find the best path forward, they can play a role in helping the world at large confront traumas and move forward in a more holistic manner.

If leaders of large corporations open their minds to goals beyond pulling in the highest possible short-term profits, and take on a sense of responsibility for the planet, not just their own bottom line, we could see a revolution in the way we conduct commerce. In some ways, this is already happening through B Corporations such as Patagonia, Ben & Jerry's, and Kickstarter, which pledge to be accountable for societal and environmental benefit.

It is especially promising that so much of microdosing culture is concentrated in Silicon Valley. The success of entrepreneurs who microdose can lead to a virtuous cycle if they funnel some of their wealth back into psychedelic research, which will in turn lead to greater understanding and destigmatization. And while microdosing alone, at non-psychoactive levels, might not be enough to push people toward consciousness-expanding experiments, people who microdose tend to be more likely to try a full dose, with its accompanying benefits.

Not just Silicon valley, but humanity as a whole has a choice to make, perhaps sooner than we think: Will we continue down a path of profit at all cost no matter the consequences for the environment or human lives, or will we cultivate a less destructive way of existing on the planet, living sustainably and working toward promotion of the common good?

Microdosing has the power to help push us down the second path.

Jim Fadiman, father of microdosing, summed up its potential the best: "Of all the results, the most significant, in our estimation, has been the new knowledge gained of the higher processes of the human mind, the framing of new and more productive research questions, and the effect on our understanding of what we can be and what vast potentialities we have still only begun to tap."

Welcome to the Third Wave.

cxli

https://www.youtube.com/watch?v=JBgKRyRCVFM&t=2661s

cxlii

https://www.amazon.com/Really-Good-Day-Microdosing-Difference/dp/0451494091

cxliii

http://www.theverge.com/2017/4/24/15403644/microdosing-lsd-acid-productivity-benefits-brain-studies

Join Our Online Microdosing Course & Community

Hey Microdosing Reader!

Did you enjoy this book? Did it help you get a basic understanding about microdosing and how you can use it to improve your quality of life?

As part of our offering to help committed learners get the most out of their microdosing protocol, we've created a comprehensive Microdosing Online Course & Community.

In our Microdosing Online Course & Community, you get access to:

–   Expert interviews with psychiatrists, medical doctors, peak performance specialists, psychotherapists, thought leaders, philosophers, and many more

–   Our Microdosing Workbook, which is an extensive workbook to help you make precise qualitative observations, plan your ideal future, and understand your transformations

–   Our premium microdosing community, where you can interact with hundreds of other microdosers to figure out the best tips and tricks for this new journey

If you want to apply what you learned in an intentional, meaningful direction with the help of a large support system, then sign up now by going here: http://thethirdwave.co/microdosing-course